6

INTERMEDIATE HISTORY

IMMIGRANTS & EXILES
SCOTLAND 1830s–1930s

SYDNEY WOOD

HODDER
GIBSON
AN HACHETTE UK COMPANY

The publishers would like to thank the following individuals, institutions and companies for permission to reproduce photographs in this book. Every effort has been made to trace ownership of copyright. The publishers are happy to make arrangements with any copyright holder whom it has not been possible to contact.

1.5 Illustrated London News

1.7 Illustrated London News

2.1 Trustees of the National Library of Scotland, Glasgow Herald, 26/7/1841, Ref 1448

2.4 Mary Evans Picture Library

4.7 [The Art Archive/The Art Archive] Boy shearing sheep early twentieth century.

4.8 Dundee City Council Arts & Heritage Department

4.9 Photo courtesy of St Andrews University Library, Cowie Collection, GMC – F55

5.3 Hulton Getty

7.1 The Scottish Referee page 1,13.5.1904/The British Library, shelf. 3980

8.14 The Vanguard, p.11,6.9.1933/The British Library shelfmark 234

10.1 © Tate, London 2001

11.1 [The Art Archive] Sydney Cove, Emigrants leaving the ship, O.W. BRIERLEY.

11.2 Thomas Faed, The Last of the Clan, 1865, Glasgow Museums: Art Gallery & Museum, Kelvingrove

11.6 Aunty Kate's Eviction, from Scottish Prose Tracts, Burns Room 74514, Gardyne Collection, Mitchell Library, Glasgow

12.1 The Scottish Farmer p.133, 29.1.1927/The British Library, shelfmark 2187

12.2 Mary Evans Picture Library

12.5 National Archives of Scotland, Edinburgh., ref: AF51/158

13.2 National Library of Scotland Shelfmark AF51/158

13.6 ©Corbis

13.7 The Trustees of the National Library of Scotland, shelfmark E.151.e

14.1 Poster advertising the sailing of the Bengal Merchant to New Zealand from the Clyde, 1839 Glasgow Museums: The People's Palace

14.2 Illustrated London News

14.5 Public Record Office Image Library Ref. CO384/92 f.15

14.6 Illustrated London News Picture Library

14.8 William James Topley/National Archives of Canada/PA-010225

16.2 Hulton Getty

16.3 ©Corbis

16.8 Thomas Faed Oh Why Left I My Home?, Laing Art Gallery, Tyne & Wear Museums

18.1 ©Hulton-Deutsch Collection/Corbis

18.2 © Hulton-Deutsch/CORBIS

18.4 ©E.O.Hoppé/Corbis

18.5 Edwin Stocqueler Australian Gold Diggings c1855, Rex Nan Kivell Collection NK10, National Library of Australia T273

18.7 Stamp Design ©2000 United States Postal Service.

19.5 Hulton-Deutsch Collection/Corbis

20.1 Image Library, State Library of New South Wales, ref. ML 365

21.1 A F Kersting

21.4 State Historical Society of North Dakota Ref E0057

21.6 © Joseph Sohm; ChromoSohm Inc./CORBIS

Orders: please contact Bookpoint Ltd, 130 Milton Park, Abingdon, Oxon OX14 4SB. Telephone: (44) 01235 827720, Fax: (44) 01235 400454. Lines are open from 9.00–5.00, Monday to Saturday, with a 24 hour message answering service. You can also order through our website www.hoddereducation.co.uk

British Library Cataloguing in Publication Data

A catalogue record for this title is available from The British Library

ISBN-13: 978-0-340-774-557

First published 2001
Impression number   10 9 8
Year   2010

Copyright © 2001 Sydney Wood

Hachette's policy is to use papers that are natural, renewable and recyclable products and made from wood grown in sustainable forests. The logging and manufacturing processes are expected to conform to the environmental regulations of the country of origin.

Cover photo from Associated Press
Illustrated by Chartwell Illustrators and Ian Heard
Typeset by Fakenham Photosetting Ltd, Fakenham, Norfolk
Printed in Great Britain for Hodder Gibson 2a Christie Street, Paisley, PA1 1NB, Scotland, UK by CPI Antony Rowe.

CONTENTS

1795	Founding of the Orange Order
1829	Catholic Emancipation
1840	Founding of Colonial Land and Emigration Commission
1845	Poor law Amendment Act
1845–8	Irish potato famine. Failure of potato crop in Highlands
1846	Repeal of the Corn Laws
1848	Andrew Carnegie emigrates to USA
1850	Gold discovered in Australia
1851	Scottish landowners able to borrow government money to help tenants to emigrate
1852	Highland Emigration Society established
1868	Ending of transporting of prisoners to convict settlements in Australia
1872	William Quarrier begins sending orphans to Canada
1872	Education (Scotland) Act
1872	Rangers Football Club established
1875	Hibernian Football Club established
1876	Mary Slessor settles in Nigeria
1878	Roman Catholic bishops restored in Scotland
1882	The Crofters' War
1882	First frozen meat shipment to Britain from New Zealand sent by William Davidson
1883	Napier Commission on crofting in the Highlands
1886	The Crofters' Holding Act
1888	Celtic Football Club established
1890	John Muir establishes the USA's first National Park in Yosemite
1914–18	First World War
1918	Education (Scotland) Act gives state aid to Catholic schools
1920s	Economic depression
1922	Empire Settlement Act
1929–31	The Great Depression
1935	The clash of Protestant Action with police

INTRODUCTION

WHO ARE THE SCOTS?

What might present-day people in Scotland say about where their families originally came from?

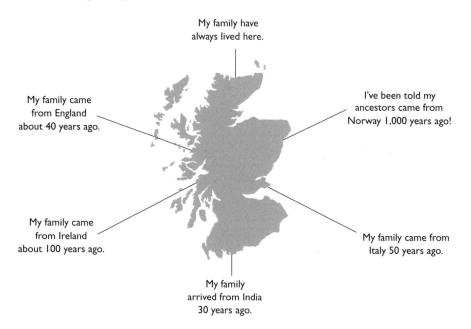

My family have always lived here.

My family came from England about 40 years ago.

I've been told my ancestors came from Norway 1,000 years ago!

My family came from Ireland about 100 years ago.

My family came from Italy 50 years ago.

My family arrived from India 30 years ago.

These are just a few possible answers. Where did your family come from? What other parts of the world have provided people who have settled here? (A glance down the shopping streets of most towns should suggest some answers.)

This book explores why one particular country – Ireland – provided so many settlers in Scotland. It deals with one particular time – the 1830s to the 1930s.

WHAT DO YOU THINK?

Why do you think that, over the centuries, so many different peoples have chosen to come and live here?

SCOTS ABROAD

But the movement of people has never been all one way. People have left Scotland in huge numbers. Of all the countries in Europe, only Norway and Ireland have sent a bigger proportion of their population abroad.

Consider these facts:
◆ About 20 million people today have Scottish ancestors.
◆ One in every 10 Australians has a Scottish name.

This is the flag of a part of Canada called Nova Scotia

Look at an atlas to see the place names in Canada, the USA, Australia or New Zealand. How many towns are named after places in Scotland? So why did so many Scots leave their homeland? This book will explore the reasons for leaving in the years from the 1830s to the 1930s. However, Scots emigrated from their homeland in large numbers before the 1830s. They have continued to leave since the 1930s.

WHAT IS IT LIKE TO BE AN EMIGRANT?

People who move to new lands don't always find life there very easy. Consider some of the problems they might face.

Emigrants usually go to countries where they expect there will be real opportunities. People who have come to Scotland from other lands have contributed a great deal to life here. Scots who have left Scotland have often done much for the lands in which they have settled. The material in this book deals with the experiences of Irish people who settled in Scotland from the 1830s to the 1930s. It also deals with the experiences of some of the Scots who left home to live in North America, Australia and New Zealand. Remember, however, that the country to which most Scots went in this period was not overseas. It was England! Millions of English people today are descended from the Scots who, for 300 years, have gone south.

Introductory Summary

This book deals with:
- the period of time from the 1830s to the 1930s
- why Irish people left Ireland to settle in Scotland
- what life and work was like for these Irish settlers
- how Scots people treated Irish immigrants
- why Scots left Scotland
- what Scots contributed to some of the places where they settled.

Emigrants to North America

Emigrants to Australia and New Zealand

Scotland

Immigrants from Ireland

Emigrants to England

Hard times in Ireland

In this chapter you will find out that:
- life was very hard for most Irish people
- population increase made it worse
- a complete failure of the potato crop on which many depended led to a dreadful crisis.

TERRIBLE POVERTY

In 1836 John Inglis visited Ireland. He went into many ordinary people's homes. This is his description of just one of them.

SOURCE 1.1

It was neither air- nor water-tight and had no bedstead and no furniture excepting a stool or a pot. There were not even the embers of a fire. In this (hut) there was a woman with five children. Her husband was a labourer. The family had had a pig but it had been taken for rent a few days before.

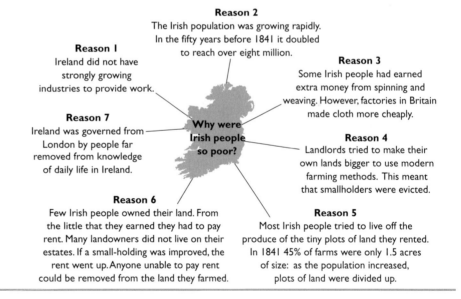

Reason 2
The Irish population was growing rapidly. In the fifty years before 1841 it doubled to reach over eight million.

Reason 1
Ireland did not have strongly growing industries to provide work.

Reason 3
Some Irish people had earned extra money from spinning and weaving. However, factories in Britain made cloth more cheaply.

Reason 7
Ireland was governed from London by people far removed from knowledge of daily life in Ireland.

Why were Irish people so poor?

Reason 4
Landlords tried to make their own lands bigger to use modern farming methods. This meant that smallholders were evicted.

Reason 6
Few Irish people owned their land. From the little that they earned they had to pay rent. Many landowners did not live on their estates. If a small-holding was improved, the rent went up. Anyone unable to pay rent could be removed from the land they farmed.

Reason 5
Most Irish people tried to live off the produce of the tiny plots of land they rented. In 1841 45% of farms were only 1.5 acres of size: as the population increased, plots of land were divided up.

WHAT DO YOU THINK?

Look through the reasons for Irish poverty. Which would you choose as the most important reason? Why?

This is the opinion of the historian J A Jackson

SOURCE 1.2

A rapidly increasing population drove them nearer to famine should the potato crop fail. The greatest risk (of starvation) lay in the swelling population.

Notice the historian's mention of potatoes. A large crop of potatoes can be grown on a small piece of land. The people of Ireland became dependent on the success of their potatoes – indeed for about half of the population potatoes were their only source of food.

Irish Troubles

Irish people had many reasons to feel anger with Britain's Government. Most Irish people were Catholics, yet various laws excluded Catholics from all sorts of positions. They could not even vote in the elections for the Irish Parliament that existed till 1801. Much of Ireland was owned by landlords who were English or Scots and who did not even live in Ireland. In the seventeenth century Protestants from Scotland and England had been encouraged to settle in Ireland, mainly in Ulster; there was often ill-feeling between them and the Catholic majority. The British Government had tried to prevent the growth of industries in Ireland lest they rival those in mainland Britain. In 1798 many Irish people supported a rising against the British Government. They were defeated, the Irish parliament was abolished.

There were, however, problems with relying only on potatoes for food:

◆ potatoes do not keep long. A good crop in one year cannot be stored for later years.
◆ If the crop failed people did not have savings to use to buy other food.

The endless struggle to survive drove many Irish people to travel to Scotland and England in search of a better life. Thomas Carlyle, a Scot, noticed this in the 1830s and wrote:

SOURCE 1.3

They cannot stay at home and starve. It is just and natural that they come here.

In the 1840s the worst happened. The potato crop failed.

FAMINE

In February 1846 the British Prime Minister, Sir Robert Peel, received a letter from an Irish landowner who wrote:

SOURCE 1.4

As one rides through the country, rotten potatoes can be seen everywhere in large quantities by the side of the road.

These potatoes had been ruined by blight, a kind of fungus that turned them into a black spongy mass that gave off a foul smell. There were signs of blight in 1845; in 1846 and 1848 it did further terrible damage. It took a further two years for it to fade away. Millions of Irish people now searched desperately for alternative foods. The children in this drawing made in the 1840s are trying to find healthy potatoes.

SOURCE 1.5

The officials who drew up the census for 1851 noted how the Irish population had fallen to 6.6 million from the 8.2 million people it had been in 1841. They reported how people tried to find food.

SOURCE 1.6

Starving people lived upon the carcasses *of diseased cattle, upon dogs and dead horses, but principally on … nettletops, wild mustard and water cresses … in some places dead bodies were found with grass in their mouths.*

WHAT HAPPENED TO THE IRISH WHO STAYED?

- Over a million people starved to death or died from dreadful diseases like cholera caused by the crisis.
- Many lost their land; they could not pay their rent and so were turned out of their homes. Landlords used police and soldiers to help them do this. Between 1847 and 1852 there were over 90,000 such evictions.
- The British Government was very slow to act. Eventually it allowed cheap corn into Ireland. It also provided some work (like road building) to help the poor earn money.
- But corn and other more expensive foods produced in Ireland that the poor there could not afford continued to be exported to Britain.
- A workhouse system to provide for very poor people had been set up in Ireland in 1838. It simply could not cope with the floods of desperate people that struggled to enter it. In any case, even for those who entered a workhouse, conditions were very cold, crowded, damp, and miserable.

It is easy to understand why so many Irish people were eager to leave their homeland.

Chapter summary
- The increasing size of the Irish population and the country's lack of modern industries meant it was very difficult for people to live a secure life.
- Because most people depended on farming and had very little land; they became dependent on potatoes as a result.
- In the mid and late 1840s the potato crops were destroyed by blight causing the death of many people. The British Government was far too slow to act and many landlords used the crisis to take away people's homes.

QUESTION PRACTICE

SOURCE 1.7

An Irish family being evicted by their landlord

1 How useful is Source 1.7 for showing what happened to many Irish people in the 1840s?   *Outcome 3*

2 Use Source 1.7 and your own knowledge to describe how landlords made life even worse for many Irish people.   *Outcome 1*

3 Use Source 1.3 and your own knowledge to explain why Irish people were leaving Ireland even before the famine.   *Outcome 2*

2

THE SCOTTISH MAGNET

In this chapter you will find out that:

♦ Irish people found it easy to travel to Scotland
♦ Irish workers could earn more in Scotland
♦ Scotland in the nineteenth century offered many job opportunities.

The evidence in Chapter 1 shows some of the reasons compelling Irish people to get out of their homeland. Such reasons are often called 'push factors'.

They went to several parts of the world, especially to the USA, England and Scotland. The reasons that attracted them to certain places rather than others are often called 'pull factors'.

So why did so many Irish people come to Scotland?

SCOTLAND WAS EASY TO REACH

The Clydeside area of Western Scotland is close to the northern part of Ireland. The journey time between the two was short and was not as costly as journeys to more distant places.

Sailing ships travelled from Belfast to Clydeside ports. From the 1820s they were joined by steamers – which were faster and more reliable than sailing ships.

SOURCE 2.1

STEAM CONVEYANCE FOR BELFAST,
BY A FIRST-CLASS STEAM-SHIP.

The TARTAR..............Captain STEWART.
IS INTENDED TO SAIL AS
UNDER:—

FROM GLASGOW,
JULY. Vessel. Railway.
Mon., 26th, at 3 P.M....6 P.M.
Friday, 30th, at 8 P.M.... ——

FROM BELFAST,
JULY.
Wednesday, ... 28th, at 6 P.M.
Monday, 2d August, at 9 P.M.

The TARTAR will remain at Greenock for the arrival of Passengers by the Railway Trains, which leave Glasgow at the hours noted above.

Cabin Passage, 10s., Fee, 2s.—Steerage, 2s. 6d.

Passengers are particularly requested to look after their own Personal Luggage, as the Proprietors will not be accountable for any article whatever, unless *entered and signed* for as received by them or their Agents.

For Freight or Passage, apply to Mr. Hill Charley, Belfast; Messrs. Kippen & Lindsay, Greenock; or here, to
THOMSON & MACCONNELL,
15, Jamaica Street.
Glasgow, July, 1841.

Advertisement for steamer services to Scotland

Many Irish emigrants had very little money; after the famine most migrants were very poor indeed. The result was that they had to travel in conditions like those described in 1833 in a report in the newspaper, *The Glasgow Argus*.

SOURCE 2.2

That fine steamer 'The Antelope' is now carrying passengers from Belfast to Glasgow at the reduced fares of a shilling for the cabin and sixpence for steerage. On her arrival at Greenock on Saturday morning she had more than a thousand of the most wretched of misgoverned Ireland's poor upon her decks. She was so crowded that the passengers had no room to lie down or rest, and many of them had been forced on to the boat's head rails. A steam-boat master who was on the quay declared that 'he never saw cattle carried with so little regard to comfort'.

WAGES WERE HIGHER IN SCOTLAND

In 1836 an official report on the Irish in Britain noted:

SOURCE 2.3

The rate of wages which the Irish obtain in Great Britain is almost invariably higher than that which they could obtain in their own country. Moreover the employment is more constant … they are able to obtain payment on a greater number of days in the year. There is more (chance) of getting employment for women and children in the manufacturing towns.

In most parts of Ireland the highest wages of a common labourer are a shilling a day. In spring 1834 labourers' wages in Edinburgh were nine shillings a week

SCOTLAND NEEDED WORKERS

Nineteenth century Scotland offered all sorts of job opportunities.

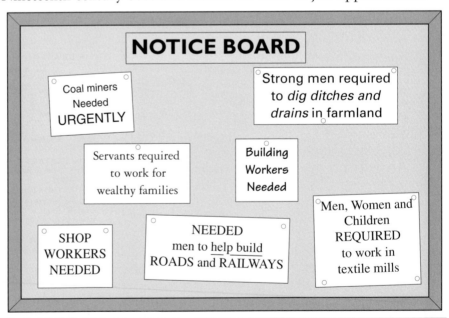

NOTICE BOARD

Coal miners Needed URGENTLY

Strong men required to *dig ditches and drains* in farmland

Servants required to work for wealthy families

Building Workers Needed

SHOP WORKERS NEEDED

NEEDED men to help build ROADS and RAILWAYS

Men, Women and Children REQUIRED to work in textile mills

WHAT DO YOU THINK?

What kinds of jobs do you think that poor people from Irish farmlands were most likely to do?

The enormous expansion of transport in Scotland meant that canal, road and railway builders needed huge numbers of men to carry out the work of creating routeways, bridges, etc.

SOURCE 2.4

The construction of the Forth Railway Bridge, 1888.

Scottish farming had been changing for some years before the 1830s. The changes brought increased output and the need for extra workers to improve the land and for other jobs at certain times of the year. John Kerr, a Scottish schools inspector who travelled around the country noted in 1840:

SOURCE 2.5

At harvest time crowds of Irishmen appeared with their sickles *wrapped up in straw under their arms.*

Coal and iron industries expanded rapidly in the nineteenth century; the textile industry moved increasingly to large-scale production in factories and produced huge quantities of cotton, woollen, and jute cloth. In the opinion of the owner of a Paisley cotton mill:

SOURCE 2.6

Our manufacturers never would have extended so rapidly if we had not had large importations *of Irish families; for the work of this town requires women and children as well as men. Sufficient (workers) would not have (come) from Scotland.*

Towns and cities expanded, requiring men to build houses, lay roads, drains, sewers, pavements, etc. These growing communities

Chapter summary
- Irish people found it was not far to travel to Scotland and that plenty of ships travelled the route. Travelling conditions were miserable.
- The very low wages paid in Ireland meant that the higher wages on offer in Scotland were attractive.
- There were many job opportunities for men, women and children in Scotland's expanding industries, transport system, and towns and cities.

offered further job opportunities in shops, markets, delivery services, street cleaning and as servants to well-to-do families.

This is how, in 1836, a Catholic clergyman explained why Irish people were prepared to travel across to Aberdeen on the east coast.

SOURCE 2.7

Several important public works were set a going, such as greatly improving our harbour, building a new pier, paving some of the streets, laying gas and water pipes: among the many strangers who came seeking to be employed about these works, a considerable number were Irish.

There were indeed many good reasons why Irish people desperate to earn a decent living came to Scotland.

QUESTION PRACTICE

1 Use Source 2.2 to describe what it was like for Irish immigrants to travel to Scotland. *Outcome 1*

For Intermediate 2 you will have to write some longer answers. They are called Extended Answers and are worth 8 marks.

2 Explain why so many Irish people were attracted to Scotland as the place to emigrate to.

Outcome 2: Extended Answer

3 IRISH PEOPLE SETTLE IN SCOTLAND

In this chapter you will find out:
◆ the numbers of Irish people coming to Scotland
◆ the places where they settled
◆ views of Scots people on this event.

HOW MANY CAME?

The evidence for this comes from the careful gathering of information (census) about the people living in Britain that takes place every ten years. This census includes information on where people were born.

SOURCE 3.1

In the year 1841 there were 126,321 Irish-born people in Scotland.
In the year 1851 there were 207,367 Irish-born people in Scotland.
In the year 1861 there were 204,083 Irish-born people in Scotland.
In the year 1871 there were 207,770 Irish-born people in Scotland.
In the year 1881 there were 218,745 Irish-born people in Scotland.
In the year 1891 there were 194,807 Irish-born people in Scotland.
In the year 1901 there were 205,064 Irish-born people in Scotland.
In the year 1911 there were 174,715 Irish-born people in Scotland.
In the year 1921 there were 159,020 Irish-born people in Scotland.
In the year 1931 there were 124,290 Irish-born people in Scotland.

But is this a full record of all the Irish people in Scotland? The historian James Handley certainly did not think so when he wrote:

SOURCE 3.2

The census takes no account of Scottish-born children yet the children of Irish immigrants were Irish too. Marriage between immigrants and Scots was uncommon.

WHAT DO YOU THINK?

Handley suggests that children's nationality is decided by their parents' nationality rather than by the actual country they were born in. Do agree with this? When do people change their nationality to that of the place where they actually live?

Notice how the numbers rise between 1841 and 1851. The potato famine is the main cause of this increase. Irish people came to Scotland before the famine to try to improve their lives. The potato crop's failure caused many to try and escape from the real danger of starving to death. The historian J E Handley noted of the Irish immigrant:

SOURCE 3.3

Self-improvement was the impulse that transported him to Scotland in pre-famine days. Self-preservation was the urge that drove him onwards in the black night of pestilence.

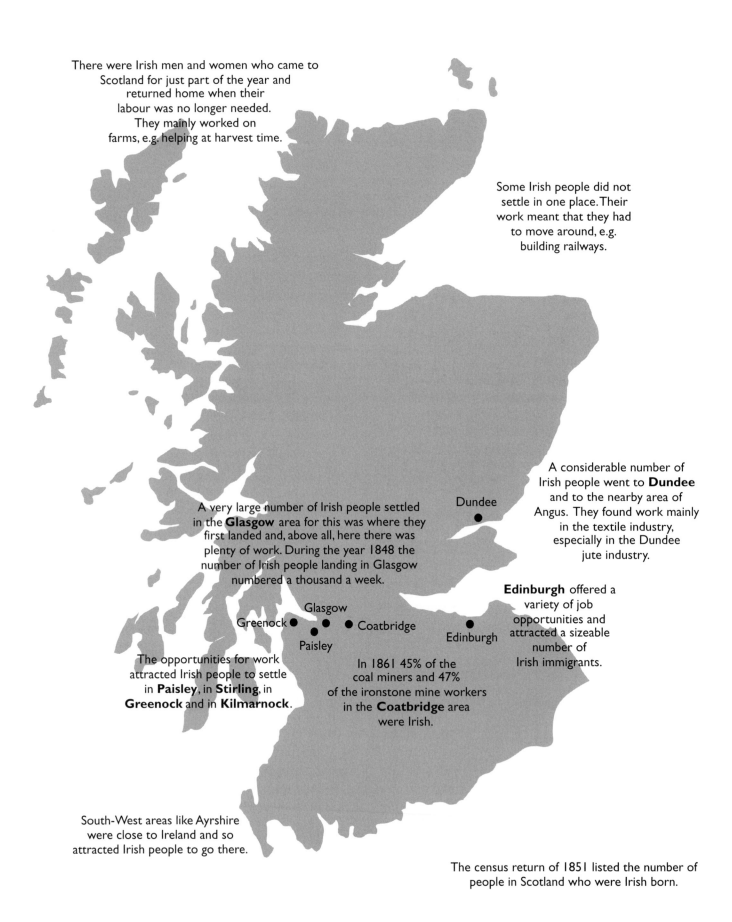

There were Irish men and women who came to Scotland for just part of the year and returned home when their labour was no longer needed. They mainly worked on farms, e.g. helping at harvest time.

Some Irish people did not settle in one place. Their work meant that they had to move around, e.g. building railways.

A very large number of Irish people settled in the **Glasgow** area for this was where they first landed and, above all, here there was plenty of work. During the year 1848 the number of Irish people landing in Glasgow numbered a thousand a week.

A considerable number of Irish people went to **Dundee** and to the nearby area of Angus. They found work mainly in the textile industry, especially in the Dundee jute industry.

Dundee

Edinburgh offered a variety of job opportunities and attracted a sizeable number of Irish immigrants.

Glasgow
Greenock ● ● ● ● Coatbridge
Paisley
Edinburgh

The opportunities for work attracted Irish people to settle in **Paisley**, in **Stirling**, in **Greenock** and in **Kilmarnock**.

In 1861 45% of the coal miners and 47% of the ironstone mine workers in the **Coatbridge** area were Irish.

South-West areas like Ayrshire were close to Ireland and so attracted Irish people to go there.

The census return of 1851 listed the number of people in Scotland who were Irish born.

Northern Ireland is especially close to Scotland so that it is not surprising that so many of the Irish immigrants came from that part of Ireland known as Ulster. In fact between 1876 and 1883 no less than 83% of Irish immigrants were Ulster people. This fact was to have important consequences for Scotland.

WHERE DID THEY GO?

SOURCE 3.4 Extracts from the 1851 census

In towns
18.2% of the population of Glasgow were Irish born
18.8% of the population of Dundee were Irish born
12.7% of the population of Paisley were Irish born
12.2% of the population of Kilmarnock were Irish born
6.5% of the population of Edinburgh were Irish born

In counties
There were 89,330 Irish born in Lanark
There were 25,678 Irish born in Renfrew
There were 20,967 Irish born in Ayr
There were 16,219 Irish born in Forfar

Scottish employers often welcomed the Irish immigrants. They provided workers for expanding industries. But in Glasgow, where the numbers of Irish were high and where local people could see the poor immigrants coming off the boats, some people were alarmed. The newspaper *The Glasgow Herald* included this report.

SOURCE 3.5

The streets of Glasgow are at present swarming with vagrants *from (Ireland) and the misery which many of these poor creatures endure can scarcely be less than what they have fled.*

Chapter summary
- The numbers of Irish people coming to Scotland rose during the nineteenth century until the 1880s.
- The potato famine caused an especially sharp rise and led to a period when poverty, above all, caused Irish people to come to Scotland.
- Irish immigrants settled in certain places, especially the Glasgow area.
- There was some alarm in Scotland, especially Glasgow, at the number of very poor people arriving from Ireland.

QUESTION PRACTICE

1 Use Source 3.2 to explain why Irish people in Scotland were more numerous than those actually listed in Source 3.1. *Outcome 2*

2 What is the value of Source 3.5 to someone trying to find out Scottish views on Irish immigration? *Outcome 3*

Source A   The historian J E Handley describes Irish immigrants' movements.

Those who preferred to try their luck in the daily hiring market at Glasgow Cross remained in the city. . . .But the vast majority headed east at once and left the town ... within half an hour of arrival.

3 Where did most Irish people go to? *Outcome 1*

4 IRISH SETTLERS AT WORK

In this chapter you will find out about:
◆ the different kinds of jobs done by Irish settlers
◆ what their working conditions were like.

Many Irish people who came to Scotland were very poor. They had to take whatever work they could find. Some possessed very useful skills that employers welcomed; the most common of these skills were in the textile industry.

WHAT SORT OF WORK?

A number of sources from the period follow. Read through them all to work out the kinds of jobs that Irish people did.

SOURCE 4.1 From an 1862 observation by a Scot who watched workers in farm fields.

Go into any field of drainers where 20 or 30 men are at work and you will find the whole, with the possible exception of the contractor, are Irishmen.

SOURCE 4.2 From a mine owner's views 1842.

The Irish in the coal mines (have) a good character. They are more obedient than the natives. ... We find them very useful as labourers: at present we could not do without them.

SOURCE 4.3 From The Glasgow Herald 1848.

John Smith, a native of Ireland who is about 20 years of age, came to work on the Caledonian Railway. While working he was knocked down when attempting to slow down one of the wagons. The wagon went over both his legs, shattering them to pieces from the knees downwards. Both legs had to be amputated

SOURCE 4.4 From a Royal Commission's enquiries of 1893.

The Lothian are invaded every year by numbers of Irish. Year after year they look for work on the same farms. ... Many of the young immigrants from Ireland have stayed in Scotland.

SOURCE 4.5 From an official enquiry into Irish people in Dundee, 1836.

They are chiefly employed in preparing and weaving canvas and coarse cloth ... women and junior members of the families are employed in the spinning mills. A number of men are employed in the works of the harbour ... but the greater proportion are weavers.

SOURCE 4.6 From a bishop's evidence to an official enquiry, 1836. He is describing the Irish in Glasgow.

A few ... have raised themselves to the rank of shopkeepers; there are several who keep whisky shops. The great bulk of the male population are hand-loom weavers or labourers employed on roads, canals, coal pits, draining, ditching, serving, masons, etc., and the female population are generally employed at the steam looms or in the cotton factories.

SOURCE 4.7

A young boy shearing sheap in the Lothians

SOURCE 4.8

A photograph from a mill in Dundee

A SUCCESS STORY

Most Irish immigrants worked for long hours and received low wages. But some Irish families did very well. One of the most successful of these was the Lipton family.

The head of the family was a poor labourer who left at the time of the potato famine. He saved money from his work in the mill and opened a small shop. His son Thomas worked in the shop, went to the USA to work, then returned to open his own grocery shop in Glasgow. He did so well that he was a millionaire by the time he was thirty.

But many jobs still had no regulations. For much of the period very long hours (including Saturday working) were usual. Wage levels were low. Women were paid less than men.

FACT FILE

Irish people in Scotland benefited from the laws that were passed to tackle some of the worst working conditions for example:

◆ 1833 Factory Act. This prevented young children from working in textile mills and limited the hours worked by 9 to 13 years olds to 48 a week.

◆ Coal Mines Act 1842. Children under 10 and women were no longer to work underground.

◆ 1864 Chimney Sweep Act. Sweeps could only use boys of at least 16 to help with chimney cleaning.

SOURCE 4.9

The first shop owned by the Liptons family

Chapter summary

◆ Irish people worked in industries like mining and textiles and in transport.

◆ Irish people worked on farms, as general labourers, servants.

◆ Some Irish people prospered; most had to work hard to survive and had to do so in harsh conditions.

QUESTION PRACTICE

Source A   Read the Reverend Charles Gordon's account below of why Irish people usually did poorly-paid work.

Most of the Irish people have been deprived of learning to read and write or make any kind of use of books.

I Why did Irish people so often do poorly-paid work?

Outcome 2

5 HOMES FOR IRISH IMMIGRANTS

MISERABLE HOMES

In 1839 a Government official investigated the old narrow streets of Glasgow. He was horrified, as his report showed.

SOURCE 5.1

Until I visited the wynds of Glasgow I did not believe that so much crime, misery and disease could exist in any civilised country. These dwellings are so damp no-one could wish to keep his horse in them. In the middle of every court there is a dung heap.

(He went in and saw the people who were crammed together inside.)

Their bed was a litter of mouldy straw mixed with rags. There was little or no furniture.

FACTFILE

The Scottish housing problem

Homes were dreadful in early nineteenth century Scotland because:
◆ The population was growing in number very rapidly.
◆ The Government had not passed laws about housing.
◆ Local governments were very weak indeed. They did not provide proper roads, sewers, drains, water supplies or cleaning services.
◆ Housing near work places was either old or was built as cheaply as possible.
◆ Many people were too poor to afford anything more than the cheapest of rents.
◆ Homes and workplaces used coal; the smoke added to the unpleasant atmosphere.
◆ Foul waste from workplaces spilled out.

Most Irish immigrants had to come to areas like these.

A journalist writing in 1843 described a grim area of Edinburgh:

SOURCE 5.2

In this part of the city there are neither sewers nor other drains, nor even privies. As a result all the refuse, garbage and excrements of at least 50,000 persons are thrown into the gutters every night … a mass of dried filth and foul vapours are created.

Poor Irish immigrants had no choice but to go to such areas. They could not afford anything else.

SOURCE 5.3

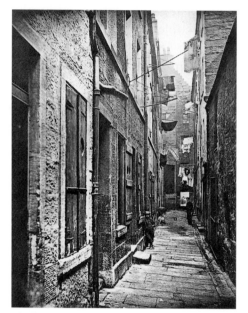

A slum in Glasgow

In 1836 two Scottish doctors reported that they found Irish people living in worse conditions than poor Scots.

SOURCE 5.4

The dwellings of the Irish are poorer than those of the Scotch in the same class: more of them are huddled together. The poor Irish frequently lie on the floor on straw. Frequently they have beds. It is the practice for as many to sleep in the same bed as can be crowded into it.

Nor were homes any better for Irish people who worked in the countryside or on building work such as railway construction.

DISEASE

Irish people who had come to Scotland to escape desperate poverty and famine found they now ran the risk of dying of several possible dreadful diseases.

WHY WERE DISEASES SO COMMON?

- People were often not well-fed enough to have the strength to fight disease.
- The food people ate often contained unhealthy materials.
- The water people drank was often disease-ridden. It was especially likely to contain animal and human waste.
- Medical understanding was poorly developed.
- The atmosphere in living and working areas was usually polluted.
- People lived crowded together so that diseases spread easily. In 1871 41% of Glasgow families' homes consisted of just one room each. Many of the very poor were packed in lodging houses.

WHAT DO YOU THINK?

What kinds of illnesses do you think would have resulted from the kinds of living conditions described above? Compare your suggestions with the evidence that follows.

BEWARE!

Cholera
Typhus
Diphtheria

These are killers!

Disease struck Irish settlers forced to live in such places. In 1886 Glasgow's Medical Officer, Dr Russell, described the worst parts of the city:

SOURCE 5.5

Bridgegate and Wynds ... has the largest proportion of inmates per inhabited room, the highest death rate overall, the highest death rate for under five years ... and the highest percentage of Irish-born inhabitants.

Chapter summary

◆ Housing in Scotland in the nineteenth century was very inadequate, partly due to the rapid growth of towns.

◆ Being poor, Irish immigrants usually had to live in the worst places.

◆ Foul living conditions resulted in terrible outbreaks of disease.

◆ In the later nineteenth and twentieth centuries there were improvements.

As the nineteenth century progressed there were improvements. In 1845 the Scottish Poor Law Act set up local groups who used local taxes to help the very poor. Until 1898 people had to have lived in a place for at least five years to qualify (from 1898 it was altered to three years). This, therefore, excluded recently-arrived Irish people. As parliament passed reforms and local government developed, so living conditions slowly improved. Water supplies, drains and sewers greatly improved town life. After the First World War, council houses were built. Yet even by the thirties many people still lived in cramped and over-crowded conditions.

QUESTION PRACTICE

1 Explain why living conditions in the nineteenth century were so miserable for so many Irish immigrants.

(Extended answer, Intermediate 2) Outcome 2

2 What is the value of Source 5.5 to someone studying this period?

Outcome 3

6 IRISH COMMUNITIES

In this chapter you will find out about:
- why Irish immigrants lived together
- the importance of the Roman Catholic Church
- community life
- differences between Protestant and Catholic Irish.

STAYING APART

Many of the Irish people who arrived in nineteenth century Scotland went, if possible, to live with other Irish people. An official enquiry of 1836 asked many Scots if they thought Irish people mixed easily with Scots. This answer, from someone in Paisley was typical of the views of Scots:

SOURCE 6.1

The Irish do not mix with the natives and do not generally adopt their habits and customs. A great proportion of them being Roman Catholic, they keep much to themselves and still keep a great deal of their national customs and religious habits.

WHAT DO YOU THINK?

Why do you think Irish immigrants behaved like this?
Do you think they were wrong to do so?

The author of Source 6.1 was talking about Catholic Irish immigrants. But a good number of Irish immigrants were Protestants from Ulster. Witnesses who gave evidence to the 1836 enquiry thought that this made a difference. This is what one of them said about Protestant Irish immigrants into Glasgow:

SOURCE 6.2

Almost all the Irish in this city and neighbourhood come here from the northern counties of Ireland ... there is not much difference between the habits of the northern Irish and the Scotch in the lower class of life.

This evidence came, of course, before the famine. A Catholic clergyman in Aberdeen saw another reason why Irish people tended to keep together.

SOURCE 6.3

The many taunts which the Irish receive from their fellow labourers, and sometimes even the overseer, tend to keep them from (the natives).

A QUESTION OF RELIGION?

In 1800 there were just a small number of Roman Catholics in Scotland. Most people were Protestants. The main church in the country, the Church of Scotland was Protestant. The arrival of thousands of Irish Catholics, therefore, brought changes.

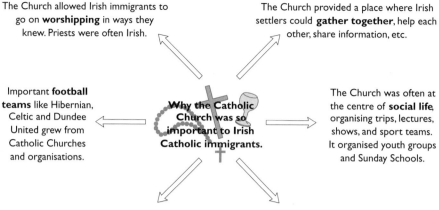

The Church allowed Irish immigrants to go on **worshipping** in ways they knew. Priests were often Irish.

The Church provided a place where Irish settlers could **gather together**, help each other, share information, etc.

Important **football teams** like Hibernian, Celtic and Dundee United grew from Catholic Churches and organisations.

Why the Catholic Church was so important to Irish Catholic immigrants.

The Church was often at the centre of **social life**, organising trips, lectures, shows, and sport teams. It organised youth groups and Sunday Schools.

The Church helped **those in great need**. It collected money for this. There were various Catholic organisations that existed to help the very poor such as the St. Vincent de Paul Society. The League of the Cross worked to persuade heavy drinkers to change their ways.

The Church developed **schools** for Catholic children. Until the 1850s Church congregations had to provide all the money needed for this. When the system of national state-supported schools was set up in 1872, Catholic schools did not join in. The Church could not get the guarantees it wanted that it would still control religious education in its schools.

WHAT DID PEOPLE AT THE TIME SAY ABOUT IRISH CATHOLICS?

People noticed how important priests were. In 1841 a factory inspector observed:

SOURCE 6.4

The influence of the priests from their constant dealings with their congregation, their knowledge of everyone in sickness and in health, and their continual devotion to their wants and interests, both spiritual and material is deservedly very great.

People noticed how important the church was as a gathering place. In the 1930s a Catholic priest explained:

SOURCE 6.5

Religion was the only security they had because they hadn't much of the world's goods and they found comfort and strength in their religion. Also they found security in that they could go to the local priest and he was there to assist them (with problems) like writing letters, getting houses, jobs and so on ... the Church afforded them an opportunity for meeting their fellow countrymen ... they were able to rely on each other.

People noticed the remarkable success of the football teams set up by the Church. Glasgow Celtic, for example, was set up by Brother Walfrid for reasons set out in a leaflet that was sent round Glasgow's East End.

SOURCE 6.6

The above club was formed in November 1887, by a number of the Catholics of the East End of the City. The main object of the club is to supply the East End conferences of the St Vincent De Paul Society with funds for the maintenance of the 'Dinner Tables' of our needy children in the Missions of St Mary's, Sacred heart, and St Michael's. Many cases of sheer poverty are left unaided through lack of means. It is therefore with this principal object that we have set afloat the Celtic, and we invite you as one of our ever-ready friends to assist in putting our new Park in proper working order for the coming football season.

Chapter summary
◆ Irish Catholic immigrants tended to join similar people already in Scotland.
◆ They based their lives around the Catholic church in social as well as religious ways.
◆ They developed a very distinct group of communities and football teams to whom they gave their support.

People saw the huge effort the Catholic Church made to develop a school system. An official report surveyed Catholic schools in the 1870s. It noted:

SOURCE 6.7

"Their new school premises are excellent. The schools are mostly large and they are doing an immense amount of good among a comparatively poor class of children who are, for the most, of poor Irish extraction.

QUESTION PRACTICE

1 Use Source 6.5 and your own knowledge to describe the ways in which the Catholic Church helped local Irish communities .

Outcome 1

2 Compare the views on how well Irish people mixed with Scots in Sources 6.1 and 6.2.

Outcome 3 – Intermediate 2

7

IRISH DIVISIONS

In this chapter you will find out that:

◆ many Irish immigrants were Protestants
◆ they found it easier to fit into life in Scotland
◆ they introduced the Orange Order to Scotland
◆ they sometimes clashed with Catholic Irish.

People in Scotland are used to the strong rivalry between Rangers and Celtic football teams. In May 1904 this cartoon appeared in a magazine and shows that this rivalry goes back a long way.

SOURCE 7.1

"The Old Firm" – Rangers versus Celtic

Evidence in Chapter 6 has shown how Celtic was set up by Catholics. It enjoyed strong support from Irish Catholics. Rangers Football Club developed as a centre of Protestant loyalty. Many of its supporters were Irish settlers too.

These Irish Protestants came from the area of northern Ireland called Ulster. Like Catholic Irish immigrants, they were searching for a better life. But they found it easier to fit into Scottish life.

◆ Many were often descended from Protestant Scots who had gone to live in Ulster in the seventeenth century.
◆ They followed the same religion as most Scots.
◆ Quite a number were skilled workers.

The historian T C Smout explained:

SOURCE 7.2

The Ulster Protestant immigrant, very often already bearing a Scottish surname, found it easier to integrate than the Catholics.

The Ulster Protestants and the Irish Catholics held different views about politics, as well as religion.
During the nineteenth century there were strong movements by Irish people still in Ireland to win back their own parliament. They demanded 'home rule' not government from Westminster. Many Catholic Irish in Scotland supported them.

But Ulster Protestants did not agree. They were proud to be British and eager to avoid being ruled by an Irish parliament, since most voters in Ireland would be Catholic. So, while green Irish banners floated over Celtic's Parkhead pitch, at Rangers' ground of Ibrox the Union Jack was on show. The historian Callum Brown sees these two grounds as:

SOURCE 7.3

The focus for a religious-political divide, drawing on the heritage of the divided north of Ireland, with the Irish tricolour flying above (Parkhead) and the Union Jack and the Red Hand of Ulster acting as common banners of the Protestant loyalism of the Ibrox faithful.

Protestant Irish settlers set up branches of their organisation the Orange Order in Scotland. This organisation began in Ireland at the end of the eighteenth century to defend Protestant religion and British rule in Ireland. It was named after William of Orange, the Dutchman who became the ruler of Britain in 1688. William replaced the Catholic King James. James had attempted, in vain, to recover his crown by launching a military campaign in Ireland.
The Orange Order spread rapidly in Scotland. By 1914 a quarter of all its British branches were in Glasgow. Members of the Order sometimes behaved violently, especially towards Catholic Irish. On the 10 August, 1875, the North British Daily Mail reported just such a battle in Partick. Irish Catholics marching back from a meeting to support home rule for Ireland found:

SOURCE 7.4

… their way blocked by a body of some hundreds of Orangemen armed with clubs and stones. Fighting broke out. Shop windows and street lamps were shattered. On the following day Home Rulers who had marched from Glasgow to the assistance of their comrades were driven off by the police and military. The Orangemen, two or three hundred strong, were allowed to patrol the streets.

In 1836 a policeman in the Gorbals stated:

SOURCE 7.5

The Irish fight both in the street and in the home. The rows of the Irish are chiefly among themselves, between the Catholics and the Protestants.

Divisions between Irish Protestants and Catholics continued into places of work, too. The historian T C Smout notes:

SOURCE 7.6

In many Clyde engineering works and shipyards there were Orangemen and Rangers supporters who thought it part of their calling to discourage the Catholic Irish. In many building firms and at the Greenock sugar factories, the foremen were (Catholic) Irish, who went to Celtic Park and (stopped) Protestant applications to labour in their squad. Overall the balance was on the Protestant side.

In the early twentieth century the division between the two Irish communities became, for a short while, even sharper. Events in Ireland brought this about. The Irish people who wanted complete independence from Britain became increasingly active and numerous. Irish Catholics in Scotland supported them. In 1918 Sinn Fein, the political party that stood for independence, won most of the parliamentary seats in Ireland. Its members refused to come to Westminster. Warfare began between the Irish Republican Army and British troops. IRA supporters in Scotland sent supplies of money and gunpowder over. Sinn Fein clubs were set up in Scotland. But the Irish Protestants and their descendants in Scotland supported their fellow Ulster Protestants who wished to remain part of Britain. In 1922 most of Ireland became independent, whilst Ulster remained part of Britain. Civil War now began in Ireland between supporters and opponents of this deal and interest in Scotland in the problem rapidly faded.

Chapter summary
- Many Protestant Irish came from Ulster to Scotland.
- They supported Rangers Football Club.
- They set up branches of the Orange Order.
- They sometimes fought with Catholic Irish.
- Each group had workplaces that they dominated.

QUESTION PRACTICE

1 What is the value of Source 7.1 to someone studying this topic? *Outcome 3*

2 Use Source 7.3 and your own knowledge to explain the rivalry between Rangers and Celtic. *Outcome 2*

A SCOTTISH WELCOME?

DID THE IRISH CAUSE LOWER LIVING STANDARDS?

During the nineteenth century a number of Scots blamed Irish people for their behaviour.

THEY SAID THE IRISH WERE VIOLENT

Newspapers of the period drew attention to violent events in which Irish people were involved; reporters often used words like 'vicious' to describe Irish people involved in fights and crimes. Irish navvies building railways were shown as especially violent. In 1840 Irish navvies terrified the people of Hamilton when, a report stated, they:

SOURCE 8.1

… turned out and, brandishing clubs, picks, etc. broke windows, assaulted every Scotch person they could meet with, jumped, yelled and altogether frightened for their lives the peaceable inhabitants.

But navvies had a reputation for being lawless, whether Scots, English or Irish. Scots and English navvies were often involved in fights too. Some witnesses gave a different view of Irish navvies, for instance as in this account by a Fife resident:

SOURCE 8.2

The workers employed on the line in our neighbourhood, a considerable number of whom are Irish, have conducted themselves all along with the greatest propriety.

In an 1836 report several police superintendents maintained that Irish people were more likely to steal, beg and fight than Scots. Glasgow's police chief stated:

SOURCE 8.3

Of the persons taken up for being drunk and disorderly more than half are Irishmen and women.

However Irish people suffered attacks too. In 1851, for example,

Irishmen working near Greenock had to escape from the would-be attack of a huge armed mob of Scots.

THEY SAID THAT IRISH IMMIGRANTS WERE IMMORAL AND LOWERED LIVING STANDARDS GENERALLY

In 1841 the *Edinburgh Post* newspaper declared:

SOURCE 8.4

The swarms of Irish labourers who pour into this country bring with them a moral and social plague.

In 1871 the writer of the report on the census return complained that Irish immigrants' influence harmed Scots and concluded:

SOURCE 8.5

It is painful to contemplate what may be the ultimate effect of this Irish immigration on the morals and habits of the people.

A writer in the newspaper *The Ayr Advertiser* argued that Irish immigrants used up most of the money from local taxes that were to support the poor and:

SOURCE 8.6

By their great numbers they have either lessened the pay (of Scots) or totally deprived thousands of the working people of Scotland (of work).

A writer describing Dundee in 1850 declared of Irish immigrants:

SOURCE 8.7

Their vile slang and immoral habits have seriously injured the character of the poor people of Dundee. The low Irish cling to their rags, their faith and their filth.

But both at the time, and since, others have questioned these harsh views. In 1836 a Glasgow cotton manufacturer maintained:

SOURCE 8.8

When the Irish first come over here, both the parents and the children are in general very decent and respectable; after they have been here some time they … are deteriorating. The change is produced by mixing with the lowest dregs of our working population.

The historian Tom Devine argues that Irish immigrants were essential to the growth of wealth in nineteenth century Scotland:

SOURCE 8.9

The Irish made a substantial contribution to the development of the Scottish economy … an abundant supply of unskilled and semi-skilled labour was crucial to Scottish industrial success.

Another historian, J A Jackson believes:

WHAT DO YOU THINK?

Did Irish settlers deserve to be blamed for all that was said to be their fault? Read through the previous section, then discuss this question.

SOURCE 8.10

Conditions were already bad before the bulk of Irish migrants arrived. Especially was this true in Scotland. ... The Irish had the misfortune to be over-represented at the bottom of social life, but the conditions they experienced were those which were the common lot of the large majority of the working class.

RELIGIOUS TROUBLES

Irish Catholics found themselves especially likely to be criticised because of their religion. Some Scots were intensely opposed to the Roman Catholic Church and its head, the Pope. In 1850 the Pope placed Catholic bishops in England. (They did not return to Scotland till 1878). The event stirred up a short period of anti-Catholic feeling among some Scots Protestants and led to the setting up of the Scottish Reformation Society to oppose the spread of Catholicism. Speakers like John Sayers Orr and Alessandro Gavazzi stirred up mobs to riot. Several publications made wild claims that the Pope was using Catholic immigrants to win control of Scotland. One of those publications, *The Protestant*, declared in June 1851:

SOURCE 8.11

If the hopes of Popery to regain her dominion *of darkness in this Kingdom of Bible light are beginning to revive, it is because she is colonising our soil from another land with hordes of her ... enslaved victims.*

By the late 1850s this burst of feeling had faded. In the 1920s and 30s another outburst of anti-Irish Catholic feeling affected parts of Scotland. The Church of Scotland's General Assembly even produced a report blaming Irish Catholics for taking Scots' jobs, spreading crime and weakening traditional Scottish Protestant standards. The report said of Irish Catholic settlers:

SOURCE 8.12

They remain a people by themselves, segregated *by reason of their race, their customs, their traditions and above all by their loyalty to their church.*

SOURCE 8.13

The Menace of the Irish Race to our Scottish Nationality

Be Scotland still to Scotland true
Amang oursels united!
For never but by Scottish hands
Maun Scottish wrangs be righted.
—*After Robert Burns.*

The Report to the General Assembly of the Church of Scotland on the Irish Problem in Scotland. Notes taken from Official Sources being added.

An anti-Irish pamphlet

Yet at the time when Irish immigration was being denounced, it had fallen to low levels. The Church of Scotland was, in part, alarmed that an Education Act of 1918 had given state support to Catholic schools. These schools' costs were paid from taxes, whilst the Catholic Church kept control of the sort of people appointed to teach in them and the religious teaching given in them.

In the later 1920s two political organisations were set up that agreed with the view that there were too many Catholic Irish in Scotland and that their presence was altering the country for the worse. Alexander Ratcliffe led the Scottish Protestant League in Glasgow;

in Edinburgh John Cormack commanded Protestant Action. For a time these two movements won council seats in their cities. During 1935 Protestant Action organised several large gatherings of its followers. Anti-Catholic rioting broke out. But the main political parties rejected cries to control Irish immigration or remove Irish Catholics from Scotland. Trouble finally ended with the coming of a far more serious event – the start of the Second World War.

SOURCE 8.14

Every League member should interest herself or himself in our new Collecting Boxes, which may be had on application to the Editor, or to the Treasurer of the Box Fund, at 205 George Street, Glasgow, our Headquarters. We solicit the co-operation of all League members, who must give their membership numbers when applying for Boxes. Give these Boxes a prominent place in your homes, or, when attending any function, take the Box with you and watch it work wonders. The Protestant public are requested to note that it is only by means of these Boxes that our members are authorised to collect funds for the general work of the S.P.L. We have no Subscription Sheets (except for special purposes, which are always clearly stated).

Please bring or send amounts collected on dates clearly stated on the Box. Official receipts given for all amounts received.

Protestant league collection box

Chapter summary

◆ Irish people were sometimes blamed for being especially violent, lowering living standards and standards of behaviour.

◆ But other groups were violent too, very low living standards already existed and the Irish made a vital contribution to Scotland's growing wealth.

◆ There were outbreaks of anti-Catholic feeling in the 1850s and the 1920s and 1930s that faded away with the start of the Second World War.

QUESTION PRACTICE

1 What evidence of anti-Catholic feeling can be seen during this period?
Outcome 1

2 Use Source 8.10 and your own knowledge to explain why Irish people did not deserve to be blamed for miserable living conditions.
Outcome 2

3 Compare the views in Sources 8.7 and 8.8.
Outcome 3; Intermediate 2

4 What is the value of Source 8.11 to someone studying anti-Catholic feeling in Scotland?
Outcome 3

9 IRISH SETTLERS JOIN IN SCOTTISH LIFE

In this chapter you will find out that:
- Irish Catholics took part in political and trade union movement
- many Irish Catholics were absorbed into wider Scottish life.

WHAT DO YOU THINK?

Read Source 9.1 and discuss its meaning.

During this period many Irish Catholics took part in Scottish life along with Scots. The historian T C Smout suggests a major reason (Source 9.1) that deserves to be studied carefully.

SOURCE 9.1

It was Cupid's darts, fired across the boundaries of sect and social strata that did as much as anything else to harmonise race relationships and prevent the West of Scotland becoming a second Ulster.

Many of the Irish immigrants who came to Scotland before the time of the potato famine married Scots and merged into Scottish life. The historian Tom Devine points out that some even changed the Irish version of their surname.

SOURCE 9.2

McDade became Davidson; O'Neil, McNeil; Dwyer, Dyer and so on. Many of the first and even of the second generation of immigrants quickly became invisible.

The Irish were sometimes blamed for difficult times in the 1820s and '30s but, Tom Devine states:

SOURCE 9.3

… there was little open and violent opposition to them in the decades before the Famine.

Times then became more difficult and Irish Catholic lives became increasingly organised around their churches. But even during the later nineteenth and early twentieth century Irish Catholics took part in Scottish life.
- They joined in early trade union activity. Irishmen led the Glasgow Cotton Spinners Association, for example.
- They took part in movements that were trying to win the vote for all adults in Scotland; such as the Chartists and the *Suffrage* Association.
- They formed part of later trade unions, such as the National Labourers' Union and the Dock Labourers' Union.
- In the late nineteenth century they often supported Liberals at election time – partly because the Liberals were trying to give Ireland its own parliament.
- In the early twentieth century, especially from the 1920s, many Irish Catholics supported the Labour Party. They included John

Wheatley who set up the Catholic Socialist Society and, in 1924, became a minister in the first Labour Government.

◆ Large numbers of the Irish Catholic community fought in the First World War.

◆ The 1918 Education (Scotland) Act that gave state money to run Catholic schools opened up full educational opportunities to Catholics.

The historian T C Smout suggests that the Irish:

SOURCE 9.4

… did, however, integrate by joining trade unions … by forming football clubs … and by ultimately joining political parties with other working men.

REVIEW YOUR WORK

This marks the end of your study of why Irish people came to Scotland and what the results were of their arrival.

Copy and complete the diagram that follows to summarise your work so far.

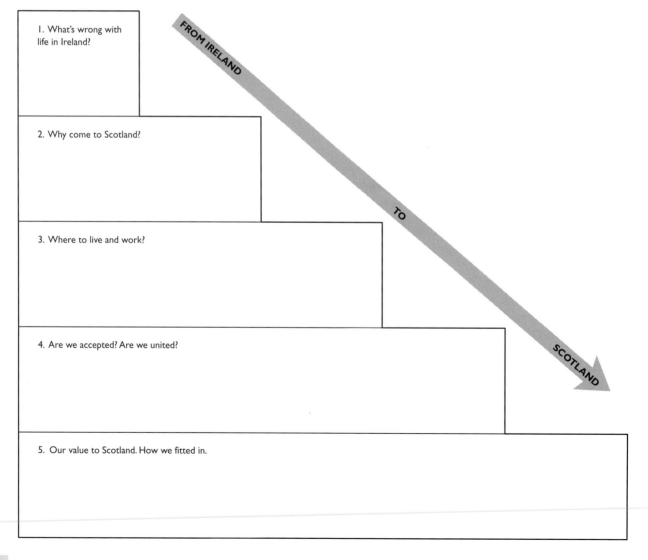

1. What's wrong with life in Ireland?

2. Why come to Scotland?

3. Where to live and work?

4. Are we accepted? Are we united?

5. Our value to Scotland. How we fitted in.

FROM IRELAND TO SCOTLAND

10

POVERTY MAKES US GO

In this chapter you will find out that:

◆ people who found it difficult to find enough work were keen to leave Scotland

◆ people whose wages were very poor were ready to leave Scotland.

SOURCE 10.1

'The Emigrants Last Sight of Home' by Richard Redgrave

This painting shows a family leaving their home. Notice how many children there are. This painting was made during 1858 but through much of the period 1830s–1930s, Scots left their homeland in very large numbers. The next four chapters deal with the reasons why so many left.

WHERE DID THEY GO? 1830s–1930s

Notice that Scots going overseas went to parts of the British Empire, or to the USA – which had been part of the British Empire until 1783.

The numbers leaving such a small country were huge. The historian Tom Devine suggests that:

SOURCE 10.2

Scotland emerges as the emigration capital of Europe for much of the period.

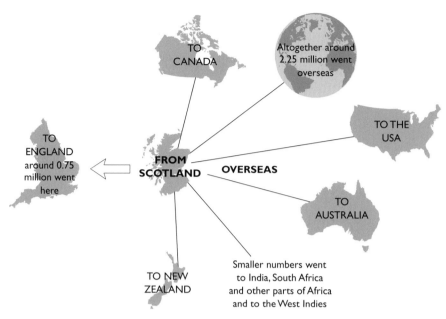

The main places Scots migrated to

WHY DID THEY GO?

There are several reasons for so much Scottish emigration. They will be explored in this and the next three chapters. The first reason affected both men and women. It was poverty. It led to emigration from towns, cities and the countryside. Some of the ways in which poverty caused people to emigrate are set out in the imaginary voices of emigrants below.

Convicts were not sent to Australia after 1867, but other poor people continued to leave Scotland. In the 1870s and after the First World War farming suffered badly from foreign competition. In the 1920s and even more so in the 1930s, Scottish industries found it very difficult to sell what they produced. Foreign competition and troubles with world trade after 1929 both played a part in this decline. These developments increased the desire of poorer people to seek a better life elsewhere.

Many of the emigrants from the countryside came from North East Scotland. From there, a local newspaper, *The Aberdeen Herald*, produced reports like these to explain emigration:

SOURCE 10.3 4 December 1852

A farm servant who may have saved £50 or £60 can get no small farm. ... His only refuge is a foreign land. And thus it is that our very best agricultural labourers are driven from the country.

SOURCE 10.4 3 June 1854

The cold and damp bothy, without a fire till the men light it — with stepping stones to walk over pools of water and mud to bed — and with everlasting (oat)meal and milk, will not induce our young ploughmen to remain at home and give up their chance of comfort, if not wealth, in America or Australia.

Some poor people were persuaded to emigrate by the letters sent to them from friends or family who had already emigrated. A great many girls in the 1830s to 1930s period worked for better-off families as servants. The next two sources are from just such letters.

SOURCE 10.5 13 March 1872, St. Johns, Canada

You may tell all the servant girls about Stonehaven that I never was so well off. The people here are not so proud and their servants live as they do themselves. ... The servants in Stonehaven do not enjoy the same comfort as the servants in St Johns although they work for little more than half the wages.

Elspet Knowles

SOURCE 10.6

So far as I have seen the great mass of the people are much better off than in Scotland. Tradesmen in Montreal are much better paid than the same classes in Aberdeen and farm servants in the country are better too. ... Those who have families have a much better prospect of seeing their children provided for in a decent way.

James Thompson

WHAT DO YOU THINK?

Some people were, by the late nineteenth and early twentieth century, alarmed by this flood of emigrants. Do you think it was helpful or harmful that so many left?

Life continued to be hard for many in Scotland. A bad winter could put some workers out of a job. By the 1930s there was a lot of unemployment in Scotland. For those out of work and with no savings, very limited help was provided after 1845 by local parochial boards. During the early twentieth century the government brought in very small old age pensions and low-level payments to some of the unemployed. It is not surprising that so many were tempted to

Chapter summary

◆ Very large numbers of Scots left Scotland for England, the USA, and parts of the British Empire.

◆ Many of these were people made poor by low wages or lack of work. Working conditions were often miserable.

◆ Letters from successful emigrants encouraged relatives and friends to leave too.

try to escape this bleak existence. One group of poor people in particular left Scotland in large numbers – Highland crofters. Their story is told in the next chapter.

QUESTION PRACTICE

1 Use Sources 10.4 and 10.5 and your knowledge to describe the conditions that caused people to emigrate
Outcome 1

2 How accurate a picture of emigrant life would sources like these provide?

3 Explain why so many poorer Scots decided to emigrate.
8 mark question, Intermediate 2 Outcome 2

11 LEAVING THE HIGHLANDS

In this chapter you will find out that:
◆ the Highlands were not prosperous enough to support its large population
◆ landowners trying to make profits moved many crofters, encouraging many to emigrate
◆ even after winning more secure lives in their crofts, Highlanders continued to emigrate.

SOURCE 11.1

Emigrant ship leaving The Highlands

SOURCE 11.2

'The Last of the Clan' by Thomas Faed, 1865

Source 11.1 shows a ship off the Island of Skye. Small boats are carrying people from the Island to board the ship and sail overseas to new lives. How did they feel about this? Thomas Faed has tried to show the feelings of those who stayed behind (Source 11.2).

WHAT DO YOU THINK?

What are the feelings the artist has tried to show? What sort of people are staying behind? Who does that suggest is sailing away?

People from the Highlands and Islands left their homes in large numbers. Many went to other parts of Britain but many also went abroad. The historian Tom Devine suggests:

SOURCE 11.3

In the early 1840s an estimated two-fifths of all Scottish emigrants were from Highland parishes.

In the later part of the period Highalnd emigrants made up a smaller proportion of the total. The historian Ewen Cameron notes:

SOURCE 11.4

The poverty-stricken Highland emigrants were not typical of the emigrants of the period.

Yet the people of the Highlands continued to drift away. By 1931 the population of the area where crofting was the way of life was a third less than it had been fifty years earlier. Many other emigrants did not really want to leave. The geologist, Sir Archibald Geikie, on a visit to Skye, saw:

SOURCE 11.5

A long procession winding along the road. ... There were old men and women, too feeble to walk, who were placed in carts, the younger members of the community on foot were carrying their bundles of clothes and household effects. ... When they set forth once more, a cry of grief went up to heaven. ... The people were on their way to be shipped to Canada.

WHY DID HIGHLANDERS LEAVE?

◆ Many had gone before the 1830s and could be joined in their homes by new migrants.
◆ The Highlands is a cold and wet area and in large parts of it the soil is not very deep and fertile. This meant that growing enough food was difficult.
◆ Until the mid-nineteenth century the Highland population was increasing in size.
◆ Many came to depend on growing potatoes; in the late 1840s the blight hit the Highlands as well as Ireland. If there had not been a great deal of help provided, Highlanders would have died of famine.
◆ Landowners moved people. At first they moved crofters to the coast, hoping they'd develop a living from fishing. This left large areas for sheep farming.

◆ The 1840s brought famine and reform of the poor law. Landowners wanted to make their estates profitable and to avoid paying out very high taxes to support the poor.
◆ In the years after the First World War, the fishing industry lost valuable markets overseas and Highlanders' part-time earnings fell sharply.
◆ Part-time work on lowland farms became very difficult to find as farmers used more machines and as farming suffered from cheap food imports.

Tackling these problems involved suffering. Source 11.6 shows a landlord's agents forcing crofters out of their home.

SOURCE 11.6 'Aunty Kate's eviction'

Landowners believed they had to change their ways if their estates were to pay their way.

In 1851 Francis Clark, a landowner, explained:

SOURCE 11.7

I have been increasing my sheep stock as the removal of crofters (made) space. The crofters could not pay their rents. The population which was five hundred is reduced to one hundred and fifty. Five of the families got crofts on other properties. Two of the crofters are in Tobermory. All the others went to America, Australia or the south of Scotland.

Some landowners provided help to the crofters they forced to emigrate. Between 1845 and 1856 over two thousand emigrated from Lewis, helped by the landowner, Sir James Matheson, with payment of their travel costs.

Resistance to landlords' actions became forceful in the early 1880s. It resulted in a government enquiry (the Napier Commission) and the passing of a law to give crofters secure rights to their crofts. Yet still people left the Highlands. In 1939 official worries about the

Chapter summary
◆ Large numbers of people left the Highlands, especially in the 1840s and 1850s.
◆ Some chose to go, some got help to go, some were forced to go and did not want to do so.
◆ The Highlands was not an economically strong area; its potato crop failed in the 1840s; part time work in farming and fishing became difficult to find in the early twentieth century.

Highlands being able to support the people who lived there were noted by an official:

SOURCE 11.8

The question is, how to enable a scattered population to live tolerably under natural conditions more difficult than those existing in any other part of Britain.

QUESTION PRACTICE

Source A   In 1851 a Lochcarron crofter with six sons and a daughter said:

I have land in which I plant potatoes and oats. I have a boat and nets. We are in great destitution. *I have sent two sons to look for work but they did not succeed. If I can find the means of emigrating I am desirous to leave the country.*

1 Use this Source and your own knowledge to explain why Highlanders emigrated in the nineteenth century.

Outcome 2

2 Look at Source 11.2. What is the value of this Source to someone investigating this topic?

Outcome 3

SUPPORT FOR EMIGRATION

In this chapter you will find out that:
- some emigrants were helped with money from individuals and charities
- some emigrants were helped by governments – both the British Government and colonial governments.

CAN YOU AFFORD TO GO?

Imagine that you lived in Scotland in this period. You have no job. You are keen to emigrate having heard wonderful stories about the opportunities in the British Empire. But how can you afford to go?

Let's see. I'll need to have . . .
- money to pay the fare to a good place overseas
- money to buy clothes, food and to pay for a home
- a job to go to

Then you see an advertisement in the newspaper that you are looking at in the local library, an advertisement like one of these:

SOURCE 12.1

DOES

the present outlook for yourself and family satisfy your aspiration? If not, the Canadian Government guarantees placement of married couples and experienced and inexperienced men on farms without charge.

CANADA

is urgently calling for farmers and farm workers. The British and Canadian Governments assist to place desirable British families with some farm experience on Canadian farms and help and advise them until established.

Special reduced rates are available for settlers to whom these offers

APPEAL

Emigrate under direct auspices, of the Canadian Government, which guarantees employment and after-care and supervision.

For full information apply to Dept. 73
Canadian Government Emigration Agent,
107, Hope Street, GLASGOW.

SOURCE 12.2

BRITISHERS!
BRING YOUR FAMILIES TO CANADA
ONLY $15.00 3RD CLASS OCEAN FARE
CHILDREN UNDER 17 YEARS FREE

CANADIAN PACIFIC STEAMSHIPS
APPLY HERE FOR FULL PARTICULARS

These advertisements appeared in a magazine, *Scottish Farmer* on 29 January 1927 and 19 April 1928. Promises like these could make all the difference. With a certain job to go to you'd be able to borrow money.

Many Scots were able to leave Scotland at their own expense. The journey to England could be managed cheaply. Some were helped by relatives – including relatives who had already emigrated and had prospered. Some saved up enough money to pay for themselves.

That still left many unable to pay to travel overseas.

WHAT DO YOU THINK?

Why might rich individuals as well as governments be ready to help pay the expenses of Scots emigrants?

WHO HELPED TO PAY FOR EMIGRATION?

LANDOWNERS

The owners of estates (especially in the Highlands) who wanted to greatly reduce the numbers living on their lands were sometimes ready to help with the costs. In 1851, the *factor* managing an estate at Glenelg described how many people were able to leave the area:

SOURCE 12.3

All of those who emigrated were provided by Mr Baillie with free passages, clothing and blankets. … Mr Baillie also sent to Canada a sum of money to provide for their wants there and to enable them to proceed to their ultimate destination. … Mr Baillie is still ready to aid the people who wish to emigrate on condition that they will embark at the Clyde for Canada and pull down their own houses before they depart.

The historian Tom Devine notes who landlords tended to pick as the people they most wanted to emigrate.

SOURCE 12.4

… landlords who actively pursued schemes of assisted emigration carefully selected those with the least resources, who were likely to require support if they remained at home from either … the estate or the Poor law. Relief of this kind would produce a greater drain on estate resources in the long run than the organisation of assisted emigration.

After the potato famine in the Highlands, landlords were able to borrow money from the government to assist emigrations.

CHARITIES

The sufferings of poor people led to some better-off people organising help for them. One form of help was support for emigration.

In the early nineteenth century, as factory-made textiles became common, the weavers who had made cloth on hand-*looms* were thrown out of work. At least 2,000 of them were helped to re-settle in Canada by charities, with a little government support.

Saint Barnado's did a little work in Scotland.

William Quarrier, who came from a poor home in Glasgow's Gorbals district, made a great deal of money from the successful boot and shoe business he built up. In 1871 he founded orphanages in Scotland. In 1872 he began to send some children from his orphanages to Canada. When his scheme ended in 1933 nearly 7,000 children had been sent to start new lives in Canada.

The Young Men's Christian Association sent boys to the colonies in the years between the First and Second World Wars.

Some charities aimed to send young single women overseas to be servants and to marry some of the many single men who had emigrated. The **British Women's Emigration Association**, for example, set up local branch committees all over the country. Their job was to recruit suitable girls. The girls who were helped to emigrate had their travel arranged and hostels organised to stay in when they arrived overseas.

COLONIAL GOVERNMENTS

Sources 12.1 and 12.2 are examples of the efforts that colonial governments made to recruit settlers. They appointed agents who travelled about the country giving talks and handing out information produced by the colonial governments. The emigrants were offered help with their travel expenses. Some were offered land and others offered jobs.

THE GOVERNMENT

During the nineteenth century Government help was very limited, though its attempt in the 1880s to tackle the problems of crofters included finding £10,000 to help Highlanders to emigrate.

After the First World War it did more. The troubles faced by British farming and industries led to a big rise in the numbers of unemployed. The Government now saw emigration as a way of tackling this problem whilst at the same time supporting colonial growth. Politicians like Lord Milner and L S Amery were keen to see the British Empire become more powerful. The end of the First World War also brought another problem in the shape of very large numbers of men leaving the armed services.

The Government set up the Overseas Settlement Committee. The Committee began by trying settle ex-servicemen overseas.

In 1922 the Empire Settlement Act provided that up to three million pounds a year could be spent on helping emigrants' travel, training and land-purchase expenses. In 1937 this sum was halved. By then the countries to which emigrants had been going had their own economic troubles and were no longer eager to accept immigrants. This brought to an end a period of under twenty years in which well over half a million Scots had left Scotland for lives elsewhere.

Chapter summary

◆ Emigration could be quite costly.

◆ There were a number of ways of getting help.

◆ In the Highlands, after the potato famine, many landlords helped pay emigrants' costs to try and cut their own costs at home.

◆ Various charities helped people to emigrate, including children and single women.

◆ Colonial governments tried to attract people to their lands with offers of land, work, and travel costs.

◆ The British Government's main efforts came in the inter-war years and were an attempt to reduce unemployment.

CANADA.

"Canada is a young country, and therefore appeals to the spirit of Youth."

___

Migration of Boys.

THE British and Canadian Governments have concluded an agreement under the Empire Settlement Act, 1922, for the joint expenditure of £1,000,000 over a period of ten years in the form of recoverable advances to assist suitable British youths to take up farming in Canada on their own account. The scheme will apply to boys who have received assisted passages, have passed through the provincial training centres in Canada, and were between 14 and 20 years of age on arrival in the Dominion. On reaching 21 years of age the boys will be eligible for a cash advance up to an amount not exceeding £500 for the purchase of a farm and for stock and equipment, provided that they have acquired the necessary training and experience by working for wages on a farm in Canada, and have saved approximately £100. Provision is made for the co-operation of the Provincial Governments, but the Dominion Government will assume responsibility for actual settlement and the general administration of the scheme. Settlement under this scheme will commence 1st April, 1928.

Canada emigration announcement, agreement under the Empire Settlement Act in the 1920's

QUESTION PRACTICE

Source A   This source comes from evidence in 1841 given to an official committee by a landlord's agent.

I have, with reference to two estates, been the means of removing a population of 1,850. They were assisted partly by the proprietor of the estates and partly from a fund in the hands of Glasgow and Edinburgh Committees of destitution.

1 Use Source A and your knowledge to describe the main ways in which people were helped to emigrate.

Outcome 1

Source B   Later in the same source the speaker, John Bowie, noted that the landlord was especially keen to see people go who:

… have no holding of land, who are mere squatters: these are the parties who fall most heavily on the proprietors, not only in supporting them but aiding them to emigrate.

2 Use Source B and your knowledge to explain why landlords were ready to help emigrants.   *Outcome 2*

3 Choose either Source 12.1 or 12.2. What is the value of your chosen source to someone investigating this topic?   *Outcome 3*

13 IN SEARCH OF FORTUNE, ADVENTURE AND CONVERTS

In this chapter you will find out that:
- many emigrants were skilled
- many emigrants were ambitious, energetic and eager for adventure
- some emigrants hoped to persuade people in other lands who were not Christians to join the Christian religion.

ATTRACTING EMIGRANTS

In 1929 people in Inverness might have walked past this building. It had been especially decorated for the visit of the Duke and Duchess of York. It was the office of the Canadian Emigration Service.

The governments that ruled the different parts of the British Empire were especially eager to attract certain people:

> **WE WANT PEOPLE WHO ARE:**
> - educated
> - skilled workers
> - ambitious
> - adventurous
> - not just poor people

People like these could greatly benefit the country they went to. But why should people who were not very poor leave Scotland? Countries like Canada, Australia and New Zealand had agents who held meetings to try and persuade Scots to emigrate.

In 1894 one of Canada's agents explained how he set about this.

SOURCE 13.1

An illustrated lecture is a never-failing attraction. ... After the lecture is over pamphlets are distributed. ... If at all practicable a personal visit (to people's homes) is arranged ... the experience of the last four years has clearly demonstrated that it is only by earnest concentration of effort that a desirable class of emigrant can be secured. The Scotch ... will not leave their homes ... until they have looked at the matter carefully and come to the conviction that it is to their advantage to do so.

Scots had to be pulled to new lands by believing they would be better off there. Pamphlets were often illustrated to make the country concerned look attractive.

SOURCE 13.2

Cover of 'The Settlers guide to New Zealand'

The success of countries like the USA and Canada in attracting able, educated and energetic Scots sometimes caused alarm in Scotland itself. In May 1912 the *Aberdeen Journal* stated.

SOURCE 13.3

Here in Aberdeen all sorts of men tell you that 'emigration is draining the best blood of the country'. ... Yet nowhere is there sign of any measure planned to stop the rot that is eating into the prosperity of Scotland.

THE PUZZLE OF EMIGRATION

After 1918, when unemployment rose in Scotland, it is easy to see why many able skilled people left the country. The prospects at home seemed very poor. In the worst years of 1931–3 over a quarter of workers had no jobs. But in the nineteenth century the Scottish economy was growing. Its success attracted people from elsewhere to Scotland. So why did people leave their own country at a time when opportunities seemed so good?

The historian Tom Devine has described this puzzle:

SOURCE 13.4

Emigration ... expanded rapidly just as (Scottish) employment opportunities became more available and standards of living rose. ... As the Scots were moving out in large numbers, so migration (into Scotland) was on the increase.

WHAT DO YOU THINK?

Think about some possible answers to this puzzle

There are a number of answers to this puzzle.

◆ Wages in Scotland were not high. It has been calculated that, in 1860, many Scottish workers could increase their incomes by about a fifth by moving to England.

◆ Scottish workers did not enjoy steady and secure jobs. There were times when trade and business prospered and times when it struggled. When times were difficult workers might lose their jobs. At times like these they were much readier to think seriously about taking their skills to another country.

◆ It became easier, during the nineteenth century, for ambitious people to travel overseas to explore work opportunities. The improvements in steamships can be seen in the time taken to travel across the Atlantic. By the 1900s very few emigrants travelled in sailing ships. A steamer could do the trip in a week – six times faster than the journey time in 1850.

◆ News from many places where Scots had already settled attracted more settlers. The attraction of opportunities to prosper pulled people from Scotland to other lands.

Tom Devine has noted how many Scottish emigrants were not from the poorest section of society.

SOURCE 13.5

Between 1815 and 1914 as many as half of the Scotsmen who moved to the USA were skilled or semi-skilled.

A further sizeable group were professional people. Educated and skilled Scots were eagerly sought by growing new countries like the USA. The granite workers of North East Scotland, for example, could earn in a day and half in the USA what it took them a whole week to earn at home.

SOURCE 13.6

Granite Workers in Salt Lake City, USA

MISSIONARIES

SOURCE 13.7

MISSIONARY
LABOURS AND SCENES
IN
SOUTHERN AFRICA;

BY

ROBERT MOFFAT,

TWENTY THREE YEARS AN AGENT OF THE LONDON MISSIONARY SOCIETY IN THAT CONTINENT.

FOURTH THOUSAND.

Preaching at Mosheu's Village.—(See page 516.)

With Engravings, by G. Baxter.

LONDON :
JOHN SNOW, PATERNOSTER-ROW.
1842.

Tital Page of missionary's book 'Missionary labours and scenes in South Africa by Robert Maffat

This is the cover of a book that was written by a Scottish Missionary in 1842. Robert Moffat devoted a large part of his life to trying to convert people in South Africa to Christianity. The huge British Empire contained many different peoples who followed many different religions. There were men and women in Scotland who were determined to convert these people to Christianity. Missionary societies were set up in Scotland to raise money, to train missionaries, and to support missionary bases in many parts of the world, but especially in Africa. Missionaries included:

- **Alexander Duff** He was the first Professor of Missions at New College, Edinburgh. He worked in India and founded Madras College.
- **Mary Slessor** settled in Nigeria in 1876 in an area new to Europeans and tried to end slavery there.
- **Dr Jane Waterson** set up a girls' school in South Africa, trained as a doctor, and settled in Nyasaland as both a doctor and a missionary.
- **David Livingstone** was Robert Moffat's son-in-law. He started working life in a Scottish cotton mill at the age of ten. He later trained as a doctor. He went to Africa as a missionary but became even more famous as an explorer.

Many of these missionaries brought valuable practical skills as well as their Christian faith to the areas where they settled. The enthusiasm for sending out missionaries from Scotland tended to fade after the First World War.

Chapter summary

- Agents who worked in Scotland for the countries to which Scots emigrated held meetings, distributed literature and visited homes to persuade Scots to emigrate.
- Many skilled workers and professional people left Scotland to obtain better pay and greater opportunities and to escape times of hardship.
- It became easier to emigrate as travel became quicker.
- In the nineteenth century a number of Scots emigrated as missionaries to try to convert people to Christianity.

QUESTION PRACTICE

1 Use Source 13.2 and your own knowledge to describe the ways in which agents tried to persuade Scots to emigrate.

Outcome 1

2 Use Source 13.4 and your own knowledge to explain why emigration from Scotland alarmed some people.

Outcome 2

3 Look carefully at Source 13.2. What do you think is the author's purpose in creating this picture?

Outcome 3

In this chapter you will find out that:
◆ the journey to overseas places was not easy
◆ conditions for many emigrants could be hard.

SOURCE 14.1

FIRST SCOTTISH
COLONY for
New Zealand

That Fine

FAST

SAILING

TEAK-BUILT

SHIP

BENGAL MERCHANT,

*501 Tons Register---*JOHN HEMERY, COMMANDER,

WILL POSITIVELY

SAIL FROM PORT-GLASGOW
For NEW ZEALAND,

With the first Body of Settlers
FROM SCOTLAND,
On FRIDAY, Oct. 25.

SINGLE WOMEN, going out as Servants to Cabin Passengers, or in charge of Married Emigrants, will receive a *Free Passage* on board of this Ship.

All Goods and Luggage must be forwarded by the 20th instant *at latest,* on which day the Ship will clear out.

For *Freight* (having room for dead Weight and Measurement Goods) and *Passage,* apply to

JOHN CRAWFORD,
24, QUEEN STREET.

NEW ZEALAND LAND CO.'S OFFICE,}
GLASGOW, 5th Oct. 1839.

J. Clark, Printer, Argus Office.

Emigrants were attracted to sail in particular ships by advertisements like this.

The journey by sailing ship to North America often took a month and a half. The journey to Australia and New Zealand took at least twice as long. Till steamers replaced sailing ships in the late nineteenth century, emigrants had to be on board for a long time.

SOURCE 14.2

EMIGRATION FROM THE ISLE OF SKYE.—" THE HERCULES " IN THE HARBOUR OF CAMPBELTON.

Drawing of emigrant ship 'Hercules' in harbour of Campbeltown

The ship in Source 14.2 was called *Hercules*. In January 1853 she loaded with 830 Highland emigrants who were hoping to travel to Adelaide in Australia. A doctor who watched people going on board noted his worries about them:

SOURCE 14.3

A large number of the mothers on the lower deck are people of a very weakly condition and the number of old people is considerable, all people of very shabby worn out constitutions badly suited for a long and wintry voyage.

When the 'Hercules' finally docked in Adelaide only 380 emigrants were still alive. The journey had taken seven months due to very stormy weather. The passengers had been hit by all sorts of diseases including smallpox and virus.

Conditions on ships gradually improved but there were still likely to be problems.

TRAVELLING PROBLEMS

◆ Ship owners tried to pack as many emigrants as possible on their ships. They were not getting much money from each traveller; carrying as many as possible was more profitable.
◆ The weather could be very rough, making passengers unwell.
◆ Poorer emigrants were often not in very good health when the journey began.

◆ Diseases spread easily in crowded ships.
◆ The food was often not very nutritious; as the journey progressed diet worsened.

WHAT DO YOU THINK?

Look at Source 14.4. It shows the food that was supposed to be provided. What might be missing to provide a healthy diet?

SOURCE 14.4

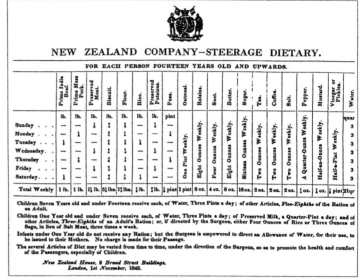

Steerage passengers to Australia and New Zealand in the middle years of the 19th century had to travel under a strict dietary regime, as this sheet indicates. Weekly allocation of water for an adult was 21 quarts.
(*Records of the New Zealand Company*)

New Zealand Company steereage dietary sheet, 1848

Several illnesses resulted from consuming food and drink that were not fit to eat.

SOURCE 14.5

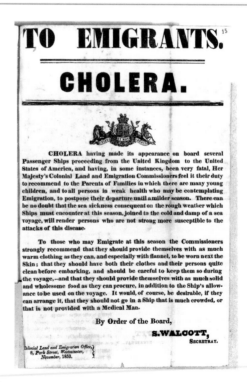

Cholera notice, Colonial Land & Emigration Office

Emigrants did not enjoy much privacy. The picture in Source 14.6 was drawn in 1844. Notice the rows of bunks into which emigrants were packed. Such ships did not have toilets for the passengers. Buckets had to be used.

SOURCE 14.6

EMIGRANTS AT DINNER.

Dinner aboard a ship bound for Australia

When John Smith and his family set off for New Zealand in 1880 he complained in the journal he kept.

SOURCE 14.7

The most unpleasant thing about the ship is such a lot of pigs, sheep, hens and ducks on board and placed on part of the deck allotted to third cabin passengers. The smells are sickening and the decks always in a mess – abominably filthy.

During the twentieth century travel became faster, safer, and less risky and unpleasant. When the vessel finally docked passengers got ready to leave.

WHAT DO YOU THINK?

What would be the thoughts in the eimigrants' minds?

Emigrants ready to disembark

Chapter summary

◆ The lengthy journeys to overseas places took a long time on sailing ships but speeded up as steamers took over in the later nineteenth century.

◆ Many emigrants in the nineteenth century travelled in very cramped, miserable, and unhealthy conditions. In some cases dreadful diseases caused their deaths.

QUESTION PRACTICE

1 Describe the problems facing nineteenth century emigrants during their journey overseas.   *Outcome 1*

2 Look carefully at Source 14.1. How reliable do you think it is?   *Outcome 3*

3 Compare the evidence in Source 14.1 with that in Source 14.6. Why do they differ?

Intermediate 2: Outcome 3

15 ACROSS THE WORLD

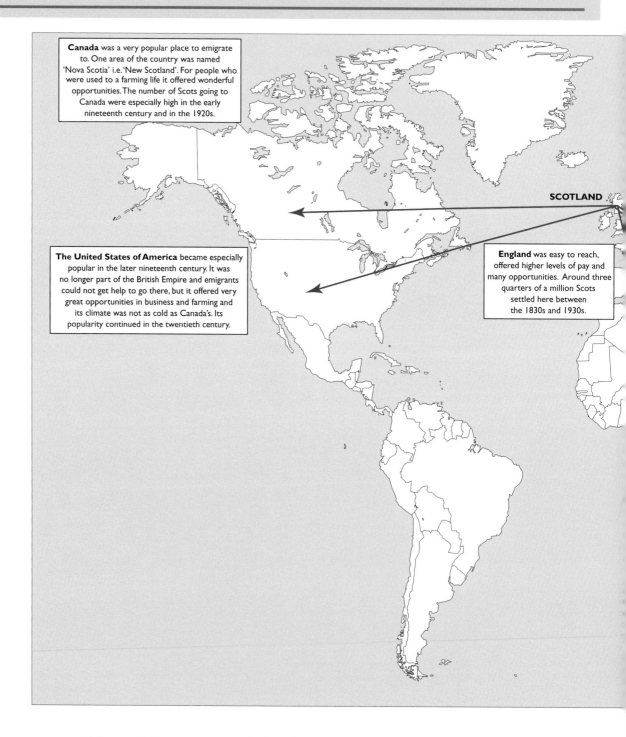

Canada was a very popular place to emigrate to. One area of the country was named 'Nova Scotia' i.e. 'New Scotland'. For people who were used to a farming life it offered wonderful opportunities. The number of Scots going to Canada were especially high in the early nineteenth century and in the 1920s.

SCOTLAND

The United States of America became especially popular in the later nineteenth century. It was no longer part of the British Empire and emigrants could not get help to go there, but it offered very great opportunities in business and farming and its climate was not as cold as Canada's. Its popularity continued in the twentieth century.

England was easy to reach, offered higher levels of pay and many opportunities. Around three quarters of a million Scots settled here between the 1830s and 1930s.

Scots emigrated to many parts of the world. The countries marked on the map are the most popular destinations. Scots regiments served in many parts of the Empire, (for example in India) and Scots were to be found helping to administer the Empire across its whole extent

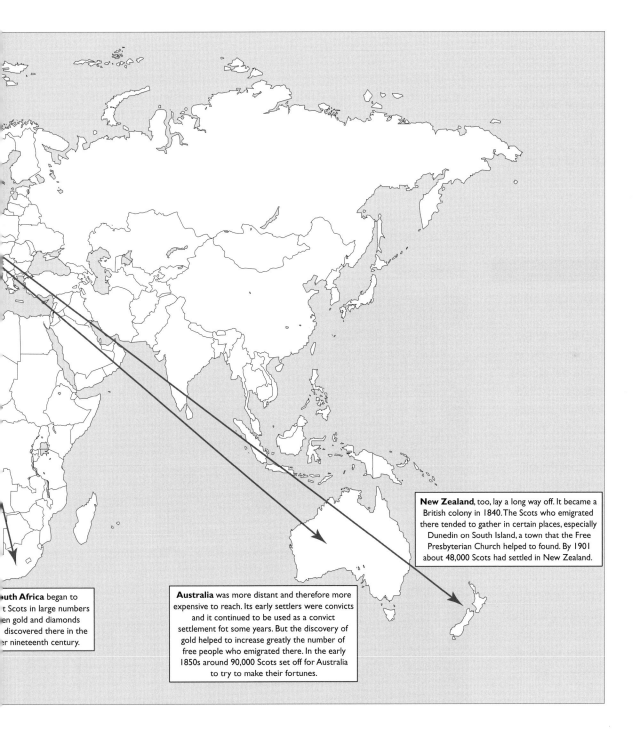

New Zealand, too, lay a long way off. It became a British colony in 1840. The Scots who emigrated there tended to gather in certain places, especially Dunedin on South Island, a town that the Free Presbyterian Church helped to found. By 1901 about 48,000 Scots had settled in New Zealand.

•uth Africa began to t Scots in large numbers en gold and diamonds discovered there in the r nineteenth century.

Australia was more distant and therefore more expensive to reach. Its early settlers were convicts and it continued to be used as a convict settlement fot some years. But the discovery of gold helped to increase greatly the number of free people who emigrated there. In the early 1850s around 90,000 Scots set off for Australia to try to make their fortunes.

SUCCESSFUL SCOTS?

In this chapter you will find out:
◆ Scots emigrants were often very successful
◆ the reasons for this
◆ some Scots preferred to return home.

In all the main areas where they settled it is possible to find many examples of the remarkable success of Scots settlers. The author Anthony Trollope wrote a book about Australia in 1873. In it he observed:

SOURCE 16.1

Those that make money are generally Scotsmen.

Among the tens of thousands of Scots who settled in England, for example, were people who prospered as farmers, as engineers, as businessmen, as ship owners, as politicians and as administrators.

FACTFILE

Some Scots who prospered in England

◆ John Logie Baird (1888–1946) settled in England after time in the West Indies. He developed many clever products; in 1926 he sent a TV picture from one room to another and in 1927 from London to Glasgow.
◆ Katherine, Duchess of Atholl (1874–1960). In 1923 she became the first Scottish woman MP. In 1924 she became a minister in the Department of Education. She was a leading critic of Fascism.
◆ David Napier (1790–1869) built up a marine engineering business in Glasgow then moved south and developed a very successful shipbuilding business on the River Thames.
◆ James Naysmith (1808–1890) left Edinburgh for London. He invented a steam hammer that was widely used in the iron industry.

SOURCE 16.2

Photo of Ramsey McDonald arriving at No 10 for Labour's first Cabinet meeting, January 1924

This photograph shows the first ever Labour Party Prime Minister arriving at 10 Downing Street to begin work. He was James Ramsay MacDonald (1866–1937). He was born in a two-roomed cottage in Lossiemouth. His mother was an unmarried servant girl. From this unpromising background he rose to the highest position in Britain.

Overseas, Scots were just as successful:

FACTFILE

Some Scots who prospered overseas

- Robert McCracken from Ayrshire developed a brewing industry in Australia.
- Robert Campbell from Greenock did so much to develop trade in Australia that when he died in 1846 he was known as 'The Father of Australian Commerce'.
- Allen Gilmour built up a huge business in Canada that included timber and shipyards.
- John Alexander MacDonald (1815–1891) from Glasgow became the first Prime Minister of Canada.
- John McDougal Stuart from Fife, a surveyor, was the first person to journey across Australia.

SOURCE 16.3

Photo of President Lincoln with Glasgow born detective Allen Pinkerton and Major General John A McClaernand on the battlefield of Antietnam, Maryland

This picture shows a truly remarkable Scot, Allan Pinkerton (1819–1884). He is on the left of the picture next to the former President of the USA, Abraham Lincoln. This photograph was taken by Alexander Gardner (from Paisley) in 1862. Pinkerton went to the USA when he was 23. He became a detective and in 1852 set up what was to become a very famous detective business – the Pinkerton Agency. He solved many crimes, revealed a plot to kill Lincoln, and was in charge of the spies who worked for Lincoln's Government during a terrible Civil War in the USA.

WHY WERE SCOTS SO SUCCESSFUL?

The historian Tom Devine offers a number of reasons for the remarkable success of Scottish emigrants:

SOURCE 16.4

They had a range of skills that few other emigrants could match. ... An added bonus was that the Scot often arrived with some capital *.... The famous traditions of Scottish elementary and higher education were also relevant to success. ... The traditional craftsman's training is now recognised ... as the key factor in Scottish dominance of much of Canadian industry.*

Even Scottish convicts who were sent out to Australia proved to be better able to read and write than English or Irish convicts! Scots spoke English, which helped them in the USA when compared to emigrants from continental countries.

The success of Scots in England is clear evidence of their skills, enterprise and education. They went, especially, to work in the Lancashire textile industry and the ship-building and engineering works of the North East and the Midlands. In the 1930s a Scottish company started steel-making in Corby in Northamptonshire; large numbers of Scots went there to work. Many Scots went to the London area where there were a whole variety of opportunities to prosper.

RETURNING HOME

In 1833 the newspaper the *Elgin Courier* carried the following comment.

SOURCE 16.5

When any person prospers in America, we are sure to hear of it; but it is seldom we hear of the miseries which many of our countrymen suffer when they go there.

Not all Scots emigrants prospered, not all enjoyed life in a new land. James Moreham wrote home from Australia in 1832:

SOURCE 16.6

What was said of the country I have found by sad experience to be false. I am very much dissatisfied with the place.

The historian Tom Devine notes of emigrants to North America:

SOURCE 16.7

By 1900 it is estimated that around one third of those Scots who left came back, sooner or later. It was not only transatlantic emigrants who behaved in this way.... The Scottish press printed articles from time to time about emigrants who had returned with 'blighted hopes and empty purses'.... However, many returned migrants had originally left Scotland with no intention of settling permanently in America.

SOURCE 16.8

'Oh Why Left I My Hame?' by Thomas Faed

WHAT DO YOU THINK?

What place might the man in this nineteenth century painting by Thomas Faed be living in? What might he be thinking?

Chapter summary

◆ Scottish emigrants often enjoyed great success in England and in overseas places.

◆ They were successful in industry, finance, farming, education and government.

◆ Success was especially due to their education and their skills.

◆ Not all Scots were successful; some gave up and returned home.

◆ Some went away for just short periods because it suited them.

QUESTION PRACTICE

1 Use Source 16.4 and your own knowledge to explain why so many Scottish emigrants were so successful.

Outcome 2

2 How useful is Source 16.8 to someone studying this topic?

Outcome 3

17 WERE SCOTS ALWAYS WELCOME?

In this chapter you will find out that:
- some Scottish settlers were not well-regarded
- some Scottish settlers took land away from native peoples already living in the lands to which they went.

Some of the very poor Gaelic-speaking Highlanders who arrived in Australia in the mid nineteenth century alarmed British people already there. In June 1853 the Immigration Agent for Victoria observed:

SOURCE 17.1

I do not consider that the inhabitants of the Islands of Scotland are well suited to the wants of the colony; their total ignorance of the English language renders it difficult to get employment for them, while their indolence *and extremely filthy habits have occasioned a general impression against them.*

In fact a good number of these people went on to do well. In general Scots immigrants were warmly welcomed by British people already living in the places to which they went. However, there was another problem.

British people who emigrated to the USA, Canada, Australia and New Zealand were going to places in which people already lived. North America was inhabited by native peoples (often called 'Indians') and by Inuit people in the far north. The native peoples of Australia became known as aborigines. New Zealand was inhabited by the Maoris.

At first the small numbers of settlers from Europe lived peacefully with native peoples. But as their numbers grew and they pushed into the interiors of the countries they had come to, they became a threat to the people already living there.

- They took land used by native peoples for hunting, farming, etc.
- Sometimes they took over lands that native peoples saw as sacred and turned them into farms.
- They began to destroy the traditional way of life of native peoples.
- They had better weapons and were able to kill native peoples who resisted.

RESISTANCE

Scots proved to be just as enthusiastic about taking native land as other Europeans. They had the big advantage of having gunpowder. In Australia the aborigines found it impossible to resist effectively. A Scots settler wrote in 1839:

SOURCE 17.2

Our natives have been much more quiet lately and I think every year they will become more accustomed to our ways. If not civilised, they now begin to find out that powder is more deadly than their spears.

However, some settlers developed a very arrogant attitude towards aborigines. One Scots emigrant, Henry Elliott, wrote:

SOURCE 17.3

I would be glad to hear of a white man being hanged for murdering a black for at present most of them would kill a black just as they would a wild beast.

The historian Tom Devine suggests:

SOURCE 17.4

… Scots … played a full part in the harsh treatment of the aboriginal peoples … some of those most notoriously involved were Highlanders who themselves had suffered clearance in the old country.

In North America, too, Scots settlers found themselves in conflict with native peoples. In 1876 Gavin Newhall left Kircudbrightshire for Oregon in the far west of the USA. There he attempted to farm but found, like other British settlers, that native peoples were not eager to be confined to reservations.
He wrote home:

SOURCE 17.5

We have a Far Western Question with the Indians. They have broken out (of their reservation) and killed a good many whites and some soldiers. There are a good many volunteers besides a force of soldiers. … The volunteers fight Indian fashion and kill every Indian they see, not like the soldiers who capture them and send them to be fed, clothed and pampered on the reservation.

WHAT DO YOU THINK?

What do you think of the attitudes shown in Sources 17.2, 17.3 and 17.5?

The Maoris of New Zealand put up well-organised resistance to British settlers. James Busby from Glasgow was in charge of settlers in New Zealand but did not, at first, have many soldiers to support him. In 1840 he persuaded Maori chiefs to sign the Treaty of Waitangi. They accepted the British Crown as the only authority able to buy their lands. Busby noted in his journal the chiefs' concern about the future (voiced at a meeting with a missionary).

SOURCE 17.6

To the question whether it was indeed true that the Government intended to seize all the land in the Islands on behalf of the Queen, the Missionary was able ... to reply, that he believed there was no such intention entertained. Then they asked if it were true that it was intended to bring out ship loads of emigrants to settle in their Country, and he was obliged to reply that he believed there was such an intention ... they immediately asked what was to become of them.

The British Government began buying Maori land cheaply and selling it on to settlers at a much higher price. In 1845 a settler's letter shows the growing Maori alarm:

SOURCE 17.7

The idea of the New Zealanders (Maoris) submitting tamely to the spirit of the 'Treaty of Waitangi' is an illusion. Every inch of land in New Zealand was private or individual property of Natives. ... Were it not that they have been industriously engaged in their own rural pursuits, and religiously respect their own mild laws, they would probably all have ere now made some demonstration that would have convinced Her Majesty's Government at Home of the fraud of the Treaty of Waitangi. 'The flag of the Queen who intends to deprive them of their lands' has been 'cut down' again and again in sight of Waitangi where first hoisted, for there the chiefs were first convinced of the meaning of the flag.

British troops arrived. Maori peoples organised themselves and chose a king. In the early 1860s war began and lasted for twelve years. A Scot, Sir Alexander Cameron, led the British soldiers. Another Scot, Donald McLean, negotiated the peace that ended the war. Yet even after this peace settlement Maoris continued to lose land to settlers. Today they form about 15% of the total population of New Zealand.

Not all Scots sought to take land from native peoples. There were Presbyterian missionaries who tried to protect the Maoris. In Australia Robert Christison tried to build good relations with the aborigines. Other Scots, too, tried to ease the misery of native peoples swept aside by land-hungry British settlers.

Chapter summary

◆ Highland emigrants speaking Gaelic were not always welcomed by other settlers.

◆ Native peoples already lived in the areas overseas to which Scots went.

◆ As they lost land to settlers, native peoples tried to resist but lacked the military strength to win.

◆ Native peoples lost their lands and their way of life; some Scots tried to help them.

QUESTION PRACTICE

1 Explain why native peoples could not prevent British settlers from taking their lands.   *Outcome 2*

2 What is the value of Source 17.9 to someone studying this topic?   *Outcome 3*

18 CHANGING THE LANDSCAPE

In this chapter you will find out that:
- ◆ Scots travelled far inland into the overseas areas where they settled
- ◆ they established farms and produced crops for export
- ◆ they went into mining
- ◆ they included people very concerned to protect the environment.

FARMING

Early British emigrants to North America and Australasia settled in places by the coast. As time passed they pushed inland. This was not easy at first. Roads and (later) railways had to be built and bridges constructed.

SOURCE 18.1

Photo of bullock team in New Zealand, on an Auckland backtrack, 1950

The pioneering early travellers could not expect to live in comfort in the areas where they settled. They had to build homes from materials that they found locally.

SOURCE 18.2

The early pioneers made do with some very basic accommodation

Yet the attraction of large areas of land that could be bought very cheaply was a powerful magnet to people leaving a farming or crofting life in Scotland. Peter Macarthur, who left Nairn for the USA, was delighted with his move and wrote home in 1867 from Iowa:

SOURCE 18.3

I wonder at people who go to New Zealand or into the woods of Canada where it takes a man days to clear a farm of one hundred acres. Here a man can get any amount of the best farming land the sun shines on for a moderate price and ready to put the plough into it.

The timber that often had to be cleared proved to be useful locally and, if there was enough of it, for export to other places. In Canada the Scot Allen Gilmour built up a huge timber business that in the 1830s included eleven shipyards and a vast fleet of ships.

The farming skills that Scots brought to the areas they cleared and developed enabled many of them to prosper. It was possible to build up farms that were huge by Scottish standards and thus to make big profits from the crops and animals on them.

Sheep farming played a big part in the early development of farming in Australia and New Zealand. It was a Scottish army officer, John Macarthur, who first introduced the merino sheep to Australia. Wool from the huge flocks owned by settlers like the Learmonth brothers (who had fifty thousand sheep) began to be exported back to Britain. Eventually this export damaged the prosperity of Scottish farmers.

The cattle and sheep reared in Australasia provided a further export-meat. In 1882 the Scot William Soltan Davidson sent off the first shipment of frozen meat aboard the *Dunedin* from New Zealand to Britain. Here, too, was an export that injured farming in Scotland.

SOURCE 18.4

Camels carrying bales of wool

MINING

Although some Scots emigrants took up coal mining and copper mining it was gold mining that was the chief attraction. Discoveries of gold were made in California in 1849, in Australia in 1851, in South Africa in 1855 and in the Klondyke by the end of the century. Each discovery attracted a fresh rush of people eager to make their fortunes. The emigrants who went to Australia to find gold helped to double the country's population in ten years.

SOURCE 18.5

Gold Diggings in Australia

SOURCE 18.5

Some prospectors were astonishingly lucky. One Scots settler, McNight, whilst out chasing a cow in a California valley, stubbed his toe on a rock full of gold. A Scots lady, Eilley Bowers, who had gone to North America, married, divorced, and made a living caring for miners, made a fortune through good luck. She took an area where a miner had staked his claim as payment for a bill he could not meet. It proved to be rich in silver.

Those hunting for gold lived hard lives in tented villages where violence was common. When Henry Loch visited Australia in 1852 he noted:

SOURCE 18.6

I was most struck by the number of vile-looking fellows wandering about. I asked what they were and was told they were gold diggers.

Whilst some made fortunes, others searched in vain.

SOURCE 18.7

John Muir. Stamp design © 2000 United States Postal Service. Reproduced with permission. All rights reserved. Written authorization from the USPS is required to use, reproduce, republish, upload, post, transmit, distribute or publicly display this image.

FACTFILE

John Muir 1838–1914

Whereas farmers and miners changed the appearance of the landscape, John Muir won lasting fame for trying to protect a part of it.

Muir came from Dunbar originally. He worked at a number of jobs in the USA. In 1867 he lost the sight of one eye as a result of an accident.

Muir loved going on long walks in the wilder parts of the country studying the plants, birds and animals that lived there. He feared that farming, timber-felling and mining would eventually destroy all the wild places.

He began to campaign for the preservation of parts of the USA in their natural state, lecturing, writing and trying to persuade influential people. He succeeded in having the Yosemite Valley in California accepted by Congress (in 1890) as the USA's first National Park. His pioneering work has since been widely copied.

Chapter summary

◆ Scots emigrants created and developed very large farms.

◆ These farms produced wool and meat for export.

◆ Scots took part in the gold mining of the later nineteenth century.

◆ John Muir created the USA's first National Park.

QUESTION PRACTICE

1 Use Source 18.7 to describe the work involved in gold mining.

Outcome 1

2 Explain why John Muir is important.

Outcome 2

19 ENTERPRISING SCOTS

In this chapter you will find out that:
- Scots did a great deal to develop business, industries, banking, etc., in countries where they settled
- Scots played an important part in education and politics.

The historian Tom Devine has noted the remarkable contribution made by Scots to the development of Canada, the USA, Australia and New Zealand.

SOURCE 19.1

In the 1880s Scots ... were dominant in Canadian textiles, paper, sugar, oil, iron and steel, furniture-making, the fur trade and bakery products. ... In the later nineteenth century it has been estimated that about one third of (Canada's) business elite *was of Scottish origin. ... In the USA there was also much evidence of Scottish business success. ... Scottish builders and operators were to the fore in the creation of the American rail network. ... They also figured very prominently in Australian business, education, religious and cultural life.*

A FAMILY SUCCESS

Joseph Moore, his wife and three sons emigrated from Rutherglen to San Francisco. There they built up the Risdon Iron and Locomotive Works. Letters written by family members give glimpses of their lives and illustrate the skills, hard work, and readiness to accept new technology so common among Scots.

SOURCE 19.2 (Part of a letter from Joseph's son Robert, 1875)

They are very busy in the shop now, running night and day on mining and steamboat work. They have just finished the little Government yacht. She was built in our new boiler shop.

SOURCE 19.3 (Part of a letter from Joseph's son Andrew, 1879)

I start on a trip through Arizona. There are a great many rich mines there, principally silver. I expect to be away two months. I have spent the greater part of this year travelling from one town to another in Nevada and California. We took an order a few days ago for one of the mines there for a pumping rig. ... We are at present busy on some sugar mill work consisting of a number of boilers.

SOURCE 19.4 (from Joseph's younger son Ralph, 1879)

Telephones are rapidly increasing, they have three in the Risdon (Works) and we are going to have one put in our house tomorrow.

FACTFILE

Andrew Carnegie 1835–1919

Andrew Carnegie's family lived in Dunfermline. His father was a hand-loom weaver who decided to emigrate when factory-based weaving ruined his business. The family left when Andrew was twelve. They emigrated to Pittsburgh in the USA where Andrew's mother's two sisters lived.

Andrew worked in various factories at first and then managed to get a job as a telegraphic messenger with the Pennsylvania Railroad Company. Here he prospered, rising in the Company because of his energy and ability. He was responsible for introducing the Company's sleeping cars. But he also had great financial skills. Finding money was not easy at first, he borrowed heavily and mortgaged the family home. His investments proved to be enormously successful; they made it possible for him to buy up iron and steel businesses, coal-fields and lake steamships.

Andrew believed that wealth should be used to benefit others. He was especially interested in creating and improving libraries. In 1808 his father had helped to found a library in Dunfermline. In 1881 Andrew paid for a brand new library there.

In 1901 he sold his businesses to the US Steel Corporation. This made him the richest man in the world. He spent the rest of his life using his wealth to help others. His achievements include paying for 2810 libraries in Britain and the USA. In 1910 he paid for the building of the Peace Palace in The Hague. He poured money into providing church organs and set up trusts to improve education and to further peace. His name can be found above a number of libraries in Scotland.

SOURCE 19.5

Andrew Carnegie

As well as businesses, Scots founded banks and supported enterprise through investment companies like the Australia Company of Edinburgh and Leith. In this way the growing economy of nineteenth century Scotland helped to pay for the development of Australia, New Zealand, Canada and the USA.

SOME ENTERPRISING SCOTS

Scots who had emigrated achieved success in many different ways.

IN POLITICS

John Alexander MacDonald from Glasgow, became the first Prime Minister of Canada in 1867, and worked hard to unite the peoples of Canada. He returned to power in 1878.

Andrew Fisher came from a poor background in an Ayrshire Village, emigrated to Australia, worked in trade unions and became Prime Minister of Australia 1908–09 and 1910–13.

Peter Fraser sailed for New Zealand in 1910, held various positions in government till he became Prime Minister in 1940.

IN FINANCE

George Smith from Old Deer went to the USA and built up banks and investment companies that did much to develop the states of Illinois and Wisconsin.
Robert Fleming created the Scottish – American Trust in 1873 that helped to finance the massive expansion of US railroads.

IN TRANSPORT

George Stephen co-operated with another Scot, Lord Strathcona, to organise and finance the creation of the Canadian Pacific Railroad.

Peter Donahue settled in California where his many enterprises included founding the first street railway in San Francisco and creating the San Francisco – San Jose Railway.

Robert Dollar left Falkirk for the USA where he eventually became one of the country's richest men through building up a vast shipping empire: he created the first round-the-world passenger service.

IN INDUSTRY

James Montgomery developed the New England textile industry.

William and Henry Chisholm came from Lochgelly, went to the USA and established the Cleveland Steel Industry.

Chapter summary
- Scots played a very important part in developing the societies to which they emigrated.
- Some made a great deal of money from their work; some of these millionaires used their success to help less fortunate people, including people still in Scotland.
- Scots' contributions to development included work in industry, trade, finance, education and politics.

Robert Dunsmuir developed coal mining in Canada.

IN EDUCATION

John Dunmore Lang came from Greenock, and went to live in Australia. He was determined both to strengthen the Presbyterian Church there and to develop education.

This very brief list gives just a small glimpse of the huge contribution that Scots made to financing and carrying out developments in industry and trade and to developing education and running the societies where they settled.

QUESTION PRACTICE

1 Use Source 19.1 and your own knowledge to describe some of the ways in which Scots helped to develop the societies where they settled.   *Outcome 1*

20

UNWILLING SETTLERS

In this chapter you will find out that:
- Britain used Australia as a place to send convicts to
- life for convicts varied a good deal.

Secure prisons were not common in Britain in the 1830s. Many people who were found guilty of crimes were 'transported', i.e. sent overseas to a place from which they would find it very difficult to escape. Till the outbreak of the American Revolution in 1776 convicts were sent to North America. But that Revolution resulted in the creation of a separate country – the USA – ending its use as a transportation destination by Britain.

The British Government searched for a new place to send the thieves, forgers, etc. who crowded the country's unsuitable prisons. In 1787 the first fleet of ships carrying convicts to Australia set sail for Botany Bay.

This use of Australia for convict settlement continued for 80 years. Among the 160,000 men and women who were sent there over that period of time were over 7,500 Scots. These convicts were gathered in Calton Gaol Edinburgh, sent south to be packed into one of the old warships on the Thames (called hulks) that were used as prisons and from there despatched on the long voyage to Australia.

WHAT HAPPENED TO CONVICTS?

- Some were allowed a good deal of freedom and even bought land.
- Some worked on clearing land and farming.
- Some had to collect and break stones and carry out building work.
- Some, who had useful skills, were given a 'ticket of leave' which provided some limited freedom. This meant that they could work for free settlers.
- After serving the years to which they had been sentenced convicts were free.
- Some, who behaved very well, might be given a pardon by the Governor.
- Some escaped (which was not difficult) but then often could not survive in the burning heat of the interior of Australia.

The convicts were supervised by a Governor and by a force of soldiers. Governors varied in how severe they were. The picture in Source 20.2 was drawn in 1836 by an enemy of the Governor of the time. It aimed to show that cruel punishments like this were used (though punishments like this were also used in the army and navy).

SOURCE 20.1

Picture of flogging at Moreton Bay

The harsh nature of this punishment was observed by people at the time. A church minister at Port Arthur saw that, after floggings had taken place:

SOURCE 20.2

… the ground on which the men stood at the triangles was saturated *with human* gore *as if a bucket of blood had been spilled on it … running out in various directions in little streams two or three feet long. I have seen this.*

As time passed, convict settlements were established at other points on Australia's southern shores, and on Tasmania. Source 20.4 shows the settlement of Port Arthur on Tasmania. It was named after its founder, Sir George Arthur who, in 1824, arrived in Van Diemen's land (as Tasmania was then known) as Lieutenant Governor of that colony.

As the numbers of free settlers in Australia increased, the developing colonies began to protest at the presence of British convict settlements. The British Government eventually gave way to their pressure. The last cargo of convicts landed in Australia on 10th January 1868.

Chapter summary
- Britain sent convicted criminals, both men and women, to settlements in Australia.
- Their experiences varied greatly, from being given a good deal of freedom to being treated cruelly.
- The system ended in 1868 because Australia was now well developed as a place for free settlers.

QUESTION PRACTICE

1 Discuss the reliability of Source 20.2 as evidence of how convicts were punished. *Outcome 3*

STILL SCOTTISH?

SOURCE 21.1

Dunedin University in New Zealand

Dunedin in New Zealand owed its development to Scottish emigrants. It provides an example of the way that Scottish emigrants often lived clustered together in large groups. Peter Macarthur, a Scot living in Iowa in 1867 observed this habit of Scots settlers.

SOURCE 21.2

In Illinois there is some large settlement of them. They seem to be like the Irish in their ways for they are very clannish.

The historian Tom Devine suggests that this 'clannish behaviour' may have been helpful to new emigrants and lasted to shape the behaviour of the children and grandchildren of settlers.

SOURCE 21.3

Loyalty to other Scots ... endured at least for the first and possibly second generations. In all countries of settlement, ethnic identity among the immigrant elite was consolidated by the Masons, Presbyterian churches, St Andrew's Societies and Burns Clubs.

SOURCE 21.4

The Caledonian Society of Cavalier County

Neil Calder, who left Bonar Bridge for Australia, illustrates the popularity of gatherings of emigrant Scots. In 1896 he wrote home:

SOURCE 21.5

I went to Maryborough (on) New Year's Day to the Caledonian (Society). It is the greatest Scotch gathering in Australia. There was an immense crowd of people there. There were about twenty pipers there in Highland costume and I can assure you my blood warmed when I heard the skirl of old Highland pipes. We had a great scotch dance. It brought olden times back to memory.

In North America and Australasia, in places where large numbers of Scots gathered, wearing tartan, bagpipe music, Highland games, Highland dances and Burns suppers all flourished. Scots emigrants founded golf clubs (such as the 1888 St Andrews Golf Club in New York); this sport was soon taken up by large numbers of non-Scots. This determination to remember a Scottish past could produce some unusual results.

SOURCE 21.6

Americans with Scottish ancestors still celebrate their roots during Scottish Pride Day, California

Intense feelings for the land that Scots emigrants had left is illustrated in this extract from a letter written in 1890 by John Calder. He had left the Highlands to live in the USA.

SOURCE 21.7

They talk about America and all these foreign countries but I don't think none of these great countries can be compared to old Scotland – provided the land was given to the people on reasonable terms.

However, the large number of Scots who emigrated to England were less likely to set up organisations whose aim was to preserve a strong sense of a Scottish identity. They often inter-married with English people and became part of the population of England rather than Scots who happened to live in England.

WHAT DO YOU THINK?

Should emigrants bother to try to preserve a past identity?

QUESTION PRACTICE

Source A   These are the rules of the Caledonian Society set up in 1871 at Waipu in New Zealand. The Society existed:

To keep up the customs, traditions and language of the Mother Country, Highland dancing, music and games, etc. And to assist any immigrants from the Highlands of Scotland who settle in Waipu and are in need of help.

1 Use the source and your own knowledge to explain why organisations to preserve Scottish identity flourished in many places to which large numbers of Scots emigrated.

SCOTTISH EMIGRATION – A SUMMARY

The second part of this book has been about the reasons for and results of Scottish emigration.

Copy and fill in the diagram to make a summary of this part of the course. Make the boxes large enough to fit all your answers in.

The main reasons for Scottish emigration were:

The main places to which Scots emigrated were:

Reasons for their success . . .   or failure . . .

Examples of people who succeeded

Name of Person   **Main Achievement**

TEST AND EXAM ADVICE

There are three basic types of question. They are listed below together with a description of what you must do for each type of question. What you must achieve for each type of question is called an 'outcome'. *Parts in italics are only needed for Intermediate 2.* The length of answer will depend on the number of marks. Try to include at least one developed point for each mark.

Outcome 1

Description questions which ask you to show your knowledge and understanding of historical developments, events and issues.

a) you must use recalled knowledge which is relevant to the question; at Intermediate 1 you much also use relevant information from the source(s).
b) your knowledge from recall (and the source(s) at Intermediate 1) must show accurate understanding of the topic and its themes and issues.

Outcome 2

Explanation questions which ask you to explain historical developments and events. You usually have to explain the reasons for, or the results of something.

a) Int. 1 and 2 – your explanation must be supported by accurate and relevant information from recall and the source(s).
b) Int. 2 only – your answer for the 8-mark short essay question must have an introduction and a conclusion (see page 82)

Outcome 3

Source evaluation questions which ask you to evaluate historical sources with reference to their context (what was happening at the time). These usually ask you how useful, reliable or accurate a source is.
a) Int. 1 – your evaluation must take into account the origin or purpose of the source (Who wrote it? When was it written? Why was it written? etc.)
Int. 2 – you must also take into account the context of the source(s) (relevant information about what was happening at the time).

b) Int. 1 – your evaluation must show you understand what is in the source.

Int. 2 – your evaluation must take into account the content of the source. You can also point out what the source fails to mention.

c) *Int. 2 only – you must be able to make an accurate comparison between two sources.*

How to write your 8 mark essay

One of the questions in internal tests and the final exam at Intermediate 2 is the 8-mark essay question.

It is an explanation type of question for which you usually have to explain the reasons for or result of something.

Remember that your essay

◆ must have an introduction
◆ must have a middle section with paragraphs for each of your main points
◆ must have a separate conclusion.

Making a plan

It often helps to jot down a list of about five main points you want to deal with before you start your essay. You can add to the list if more points occur to you.

Introduction: This is worth 1 or 2 marks.

It should deal with the question. It might only be a sentence or two. You could start with a sentence like this: '*There were many reasons why . . . (such and such happened). These reasons were . . .*

Middle section. This is worth 5 marks.

If you have five main points you should have five paragraphs in the middle section of your essay.

Each paragraph should start with a sentence which sets out what the paragraph will be about. You should then explain what your main point means or how it is connected to the question.

You then go on to use accurate and relevant facts to explain what you mean and show off what you know.

Conclusion. This is worth 1 or 2 marks.

It should be a paragraph of a few sentences.

It should sum up your answer. It could be something like this – '*In conclusion, there were lots of reasons why . . . (such and such happened) These reasons included . . . (sum up your main points).*'

In your conclusion you should:

◆ Sum up the points you have explained earlier in the answer. You could also say which points you think were the most important and give reasons.
◆ Make up your mind and answer the question that you were asked.

Use this pattern for all your 8 mark essays. You can also use it to help you with your extended response. Remember you only have to do one 8 mark essay in the exam. Use the advice on this page to get it right.

The following example shows how an 8 mark essay can be organised. The question is:

Why did so many Scots emigrate in the nineteenth century?

Introduction

You could start with a sentence like this:

There are several reasons why Scots left their homeland in the nineteenth century. These reasons were ...
Then briefly summarise them.

Middle section

Here you need a paragraph for each of the reasons mentioned in your introduction. Each paragraph could start with a main sentence that says what the paragraph will be about.
Your first paragraph could start like this:

The first reason why so many Scots emigrated was the low wages paid to Scottish workers.

Use your knowledge to explain this more fully. Then go on to the next reason. You might choose, for example, to deal with the Highland Clearances next. Take each reason in turn in this way.

Conclusion

Your conclusion should sum up your answer. It could be something like this;

There were many causes of Scottish emigration. They vary greatly, for some emigrants were eager to leave and were pulled by the hope of a better and more prosperous life elsewhere. Some found higher wages in England. Some were eager to get their own land or set up their own business overseas. Some were glad to escape a miserable life at home and welcomed any opportunity on offer. But others did not wish to leave. They included convicts and Highlanders forced to leave their homes. All helped to greatly change the places to which they went.

A conclusion like this brings together the main points in a very clear way and directly answers the question. Now try to write a full answer to the question above.

EXTENDED RESPONSE ADVICE

Intermediate 2 candidates must also produce a longer prepared essay as part of the external course assessment – usually round about February/March.

This is called the Extended Response and is worth one quarter of the final marks. It is similar to the 8-mark short essay (see page 82). The main differences are:

◆ It will be much longer than an 8-mark short essay. You will have an hour to write it. It could be up to 1000 words long (four or fives sides of A4).

◆ You choose your own question relating to one of the three units making up your course. Your teacher can advise you on this.

◆ You research and prepare your answer by reading and taking notes from a variety of sources. Your teacher can help you with sources.

◆ You prepare a plan of 150 words with sub-headings which you can take into the final writing-up session. Your teacher can check your plan for you.

◆ A teacher will supervise the final one-hour writing-up session under exam conditions, but cannot help you in any way. Your plan and response are then sent to the SQA for marking.

CHOOSING A QUESTION

◆ Pick a topic that interests you and the you feel you can do well in.

◆ Discuss the exact wording of the question with your teacher.

◆ Choose a question that requires you to explain and assess what happened rather than simply describing events.

◆ Avoid questions which cover too much or which are too vague or too narrow.

◆ You should be able to divide it up into about five sub-headings.

◆ Some possible questions for this unit are given on the next page.

READING AND NOTE-TAKING

Talk to your teacher about sources.

As you read, jot down notes for your different sub-headings (either using separate sheets for each sub-heading or by indicating in the margin which sub-heading each note is about). Use key words and avoid copying whole sentences and paragraphs – try to use one or two good short 'quotes'.

PREPARING YOUR PLAN

Use your notes to prepare your 150 word plan.
This should consist of sub-headings and key points to remind you of what you want to include.
You could also draw a spider diagram like the one on the next page to help you.

If you want, you can write a practise draft of your full response, but you cannot take it into the final write-up session with you.
You are only allowed to take in your plan of not more than 150 words.

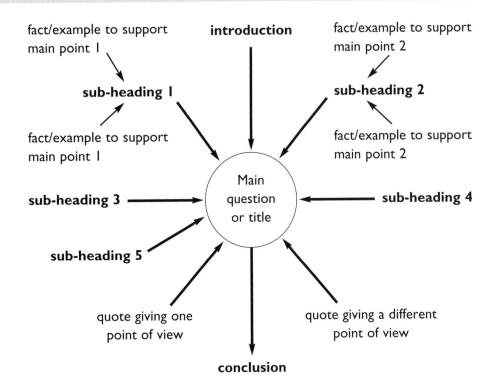

	introduction	
fact/example to support main point 1		fact/example to support main point 2
sub-heading 1		**sub-heading 2**
fact/example to support main point 1		fact/example to support main point 2
sub-heading 3	Main question or title	**sub-heading 4**
sub-heading 5		
quote giving one point of view		quote giving a different point of view
	conclusion	

THE WRITE-UP SESSION

Your plan will enable you to work your way steadily through your response.

You have one hour to do this, allowing about ten minutes for each sub-heading and leaving time for your conclusion.

Try to concentrate on explanation and analysis rather than just description and narrative.

If you are running out of time, make quick notes about any remaining sub-headings and go straight to your conclusion.

POSSIBLE EXTENDED RESPONSE QUESTIONS

- Why did so many Irish people come to Scotland?
- How important were the Highland Clearances in causing emigration?
- What difficulties faced Irish people settling in Scotland?
- What did Scots contribute to the development of either Canada or Australia?
- In what ways and for what reasons were people helped to emigrate from Scotland?
- For what does Andrew Carnegie deserve to be remembered?
- To what extent and for what reasons were the Irish a separate community in Scotland?
- Was poverty the main reason for Scottish emigration?
- Did Irish immigrants to Scotland deserve the criticisms that they received?

- How did Irish immigration affect the development of football clubs in Scotland?
- What kinds of lives were lived by Scots sent to Australia as convicts?
- In what ways and for what reasons did emigrant Scots try to preserve a Scottish identity?
- To what extent did Scottish emigrants damage the lives lived by native peoples in the lands where they settled?
- Why were so many Scottish emigrants so successful in the lands where they settled?
- Was Scottish emigration in the 1920s and 1930s chiefly caused by unemployment?

A NOTE ON SOURCES

PRIMARY SOURCES

The Scottish Record Office (SRO) and the National Library of Scotland, both in Edinburgh, hold many sources for studying migration. The SRO has an Education officer who should be contacted before making a visit.

The SRO has published several very useful booklets that contain helpful sources and refer to others that it holds. These booklets consists of:

The Scots in New Zealand (1994)
The Scots in Australia (1994)
The Scots in America (1994)
The Emigrants (1994)
The Scots in Canada (1994)

Contact the SRO at H M General Register House, Princes Street, Edinburgh EH1 3YY.

Official reports and parliamentary enquiries can be found in major libraries. Especially useful are *The Report on the State of the Irish Poor in Britain, 1836* and *The Report on Empire Migration, 1932*.

Newspapers can be very useful for the letters, reports and advertisements that they contain. Main local libraries hold the papers for each local area.

Personal accounts can be difficult to obtain, but some have been published, for example:
Robert MacDougall, *The Emigrant's Guide to North America*; first published in 1841 it has been reissued in 1998 by Natural Heritage.
Ann Anderson, *Memoirs of a Country Lass from Aberdeenshire to Australia* 1992 Penland Press
Robert Somers, *Letters from the Highlands on the Famine of 1846* 1985

SECONDARY SOURCES

These often include short extracts from primary sources.

CD ROMs
Immigrants and Exiles
Saints and Sinners – the Scots in Australia
both from Dunedin Multimedia

Video
The Scots Detective Channel 4, 2000

Books

Mona McLeod, *Leaving Scotland* National Museum 1996 (This provides a clear, brief overall survey)

T M Devine (ed), *Scottish Emigration and Scottish Society* J Donald, 1992 (This is a useful collection of academic essays).

That Land of Exiles. Scots in Australia H M Stationery Office 1998. (This is a useful, quite accessible and well-illustrated survey)

Tom Bryan, *Rich Man, Beggar Man, Indian Chief. Fascinating Scots in Canada and America*, Thistle 1997 (This consists of numerous short and very readable biographies)

T M Devine, *The Scottish Nation* Penguin 1999 (A clearly written and invaluable survey of Scotland with much of relevance in it.

T C Smout, *A Century of the Scottish People* Collins-Fontana 1986 (A most readable survey covering circumstances in Scotland)

James Handley's two books on the Irish in Scotland are most useful and have many source extracts in them. They are both, alas, out of print. They are:
The Irish in Scotland 1798–1845, Cork University Press 1943
The Irish in Modern Scotland Cork University Press 1938

Malcolm Gray, *Scots on the Move* Scottish Social and Economic History Society (This is a useful pamphlet about migration; it is written in a rather academic style)

Michael Brander, *The Emigrant Scots* Constable 1982 (This is a useful outline survey)

Marjory Harper, *Emigration from North East Scotland* Aberdeen University Press 1988 (This very detailed account consists of two volumes)

T M Devine, *Clanship to Crofters* Manchester University Press 1994 (A very useful study of Highland conditions)

The above works have valuable bibliographies in them that can be searched for further works.

GLOSSARY

amputated	having a leg or arm cut off
bothy	a small outhouse or room over a stable to house *workers*
capital	wealth
carcasses	bodies of dead animals
census	an official count of the population
destitution	very great poverty
dominion	rule, authority
elite	the most powerful or wealthy people
embers	glowing pieces of fuel in a dying fire
ethnic identity	being part of a common group who share ideas, beliefs
factor	the manager of an estate
gore	blood from a wound
importations	bringing goods in
indolence	laziness
inmates	people who live in or are forced to live in a building
looms	machines for weaving cloth
Masons	Members of the Society of Freemasons
overseer	a person who supervises others
pestilence	a dreadful disease
privies	toilets
propriety	behaving properly, to fit in with others
saturated	absolutely soaked through
segregated	separated
sickle	curved-bladed tool for cutting corn
small holding	small area of farmland
strata	layers
suffrage	the right to vote
taunts	critical jeering remarks
vagrants	people without homes who wander about
wynds	narrow lanes

INDEX